Day

Edited by **Jackie Harris**   January–April 2023

6 **Contentment**
Catherine Larner   *1–14 January*

21 **Using the armour of God (Ephesians 6)**
Di Archer   *15–21 January*

29 **God's view of work**
Amy Boucher Pye   *22 January–4 February*

44 **People like us (1 Corinthians)**
Sheila Jacobs   *5–18 February*

59 **Walking the wilderness with God**
Rachel Turner   *19 February–4 March*

74 **Tending the mind**
Sandra Wheatley   *5–11 March*

82 **The wives of the patriarchs**
Elaine Storkey   *12–25 March*

97 **What Jesus said in his final hours**
Lyndall Bywater   *26 March–8 April*

112 **Igniting hope**
Catherine Butcher   *9–22 April*

127 **The cloud of witnesses**
Chris Leonard   *23–30 April*

Writers in this issue

Catherine Larner is a freelance writer, editor and presenter. She reports on literature, culture and faith for national, regional and Christian magazines and local radio.

Di Archer is CEO of **tastelifeuk.org**, a charity she cofounded after her family's experience of eating disorders. An educator, writer and speaker, she is also resources manager on the CPAS leadership training team.

Amy Boucher Pye is a writer, speaker and spiritual director who runs the *Woman Alive* book club. She's the author of several books, including *Celebrating Christmas* (BRF, 2021). Find her at **amyboucherpye.com**.

Sheila Jacobs is a writer, editor and an award-winning author. She lives in rural north Essex, attends an Elim church where she serves as deacon and is a day chaplain at a retreat centre.

Rachel Turner is an author and speaker and the pioneer of Parenting for Faith. Until March 2022, she led the Parenting for Faith team at BRF, and she presents the Parenting for Faith course, a video-based resource for church groups and individuals.

Sandra Wheatley lives in Newcastle and loves to share God's encouragements through her writing and extensive prayer ministry. Due to the rapid onset of MS, retirement from her nursing career came early.

Elaine Storkey is an academic, author, broadcaster and senior member of Newnham College, Cambridge. A former president of Tearfund, she also directed the London Institute for Contemporary Christianity for ten years and has taught in universities both in the UK and overseas.

Lyndall Bywater lives in Canterbury and works with The Salvation Army and the diocese of Canterbury, helping people pray. She is the author of two books, both published by BRF: *Faith in the Making* (2018) and *Prayer in the Making* (2019).

Catherine Butcher is a freelance writer and editor, an Anglican reader and a member of General Synod. As communications director for HOPE Together for ten years, she wrote magazines and books to help churches make Jesus known.

Chris Leonard has been writing for *Day by Day with God* since 1998 and has several books published by BRF. She leads writing groups, creative writing holidays and a church homegroup, and has three young grandchildren.

Welcome

We're so pleased that you have joined us at the beginning of 2023. You are in the company of women who know the Bible to be a source of strength and inspiration for life, and we hope these studies will encourage you and spur you on in your faith journey.

At the beginning of this new year, I wonder where you are at and how you are feeling. Some of us may be hopeful, looking joyfully to the year ahead. Others perhaps are wary, with concerns about what might happen or simply weighed down with burdens that have accumulated over the last twelve months.

As I have read through the studies in this edition, I am drawn again and again to the truth that when we belong to Jesus, we are secure in him whatever our circumstances.

We begin with a study on contentment, how to use the armour of God and what God's view of work can teach us. We will be delving into 1 Corinthians, with its call to love and respect all of God's people, exploring what God might be doing through tough seasons in our lives and learning how to care for our mental well-being. The patriarchs' wives will teach us how God can use us despite our failings, and we will be considering who our influences are and how we might influence others.

As we draw closer to Easter, our studies focus on Jesus, what he has done for us, the hope we have and how we might share it. Perhaps there is something in this list that resonates with you. If so, turn to that study first and let God minister to you through his word.

Some of the teaching may challenge us, but we have God's promise that he is working in us to give us 'the desire and the power to do what pleases him' (Philippians 2:13, NLT). We just need to be willing to let him lead us step by step. Perhaps if we're thinking of New Year's resolutions, that's a good one to make.

So, as we begin these studies together, let's make these words from the letter to the Hebrews our prayer for 2023: 'May the God of peace... equip [us] with all [we] need for doing his will. May he produce in [us], through the power of Jesus Christ, every good thing that is pleasing to him' (Hebrews 13:20–21, NLT).

Jackie Harris, Editor

Contentment

Catherine Larner writes:

The start of another year can bring mixed emotions. I know that I am full of anticipation at what the next twelve months will bring, and delight in the potential when I open a clean, crisp and empty diary. But I also cannot avoid the fact that many of the things I'm hoping for in the year ahead are much the same as those I wished for last year. Instead of celebrating continuing good health, a home, a job, and the love and support of friends and family, there is still the niggling sensation that ambitions and dreams haven't been fulfilled.

What is it about us that means we always long for something more and are never truly satisfied with what we have? And why do we assume that something better is always out of reach, rather than delight in how much we have been blessed?

Advertising constantly urges us to possess the newest, the biggest and the brightest. In the western world, our economy is based on our always wanting to acquire more – more money, more possessions, more status.

We've all probably had an idea of what would bring us contentment. I can look back on the time when I thought a new job would bring a sense of achievement and fulfilment. And then when struggling with a family illness, I vowed never to take health for granted again.

But what if you get your heart's desire, will you find yourself yearning for something else? And what if a difficult situation isn't resolved, how do you cope? As long as we look to belongings or circumstances for satisfaction, we are unlikely ever to be content with what we have.

Throughout the Bible we are urged to look not at our external situation but to our relationship with God. Because of what Jesus has done for us on the cross we are freed from sin, assured of salvation and guaranteed a place in heaven. The big things have been taken care of.

While it's not wrong to want things we don't have or to be troubled by illness or hardship, it's important not to be controlled by those feelings and to have a different perspective on what matters. In Philippians, Paul tells us that he has learned to be content in all circumstances. Can we do the same?

What is contentment?

For we brought nothing into the world, and we can take nothing out of it. But if we have food and clothing, we will be content with that. (NIV)

It should be easy, shouldn't it? To be satisfied with what we have, who we are and where we are. After all, life in our western world is, on the whole, full of unprecedented riches in a time of relative peace and stability.

I am regularly bewildered by the choice of yoghurts in the supermarket, clothes stores changing their ranges weekly and the infinite array of leisure activities for our entertainment. Those of us living in the west often have a fear of missing out. We want the things our neighbour has, and we believe the sales pitch that the 'next big thing' will make our life so much better.

It is not wrong to wish for all that life can offer – Jesus said that he wanted us to live life to the full – but contentment comes from giving these things the right priority.

It is not about denying our desires for things we cannot have, but rather not being controlled by those feelings. We shouldn't pretend things are right when they're not, but we should be able to accept the situation and trust God to work out problems for our good. And it isn't about always being happy but in having joy in all circumstances, knowing God is in control.

Contentment is not about achieving what we want but realising how much we already have. It is an attitude of mind and heart, of looking upwards rather than outwards for meaning, purpose and satisfaction.

The theologian John Stott wrote: 'Contentment is the secret of inward peace. It remembers the stark truth that we brought nothing into the world and we can take nothing out of it... Our enemy is not possessions, but excess. Our battle cry is not "Nothing!" but "Enough!"... Simplicity says, if we have food and clothing, we will be content with that.'

Lord, help me to accept where I am today in this moment, rather than thinking about the year ahead or times past. Thank you, Lord, that you have given me everything I need. Amen

CATHERINE LARNER

7

Human nature

I've decided that there's nothing better to do than go ahead and have a good time and get the most we can out of life. That's it – eat, drink, and make the most of your job. It's God's gift. (MSG)

Before we beat ourselves up about how we've been given much but still fail ourselves and God in not being content with our lives today, we need to acknowledge that we are contending with an inherent character trait. Let's think back to Adam and Eve. Despite them being given a paradise of companionship, sustenance and beauty, they wanted the one thing which was off limits. Their greed and desire had far-reaching consequences for all humankind, as the close relationship between God and his creation was broken.

Generally, people have been striving ever since for more possessions, more land, more wealth in the quest to find a purpose for life. Because without God, this is all there is.

What's more, according to the teacher writing in Ecclesiastes, God has given us a desire for beauty, immortality and knowledge that cannot be satisfied on earth (3:10–11). We can't find contentment in this world alone, says the teacher, because God doesn't want us to. If we were satisfied with this world, then we wouldn't seek him.

The teacher thinks he has experienced all that the world has to offer. He has wealth, wisdom and fame. He has achieved much in his life, and he has lived in a time of peace. He realises that everything is a gift from God, yet 'under the sun', that is, on earth, he says that all is 'meaningless' (NIV).

He concludes that it is right that we should keep wanting more – it means that we push ourselves to invent, to create, to better our lives for ourselves and others (11:1–2) and to make the most of every moment. But our dissatisfaction should also mean that we start looking for God.

Think of anyone you know who is mindful of the futility of their existence and despairing of the meaninglessness of life. Pray that they might see something of God in the world and seek a relationship with him.

CATHERINE LARNER

Living life to the full

'I have come that they may have life, and have it to the full.' (NIV)

It's wonderful that we don't have to experience the 'meaningless' existence described by the teacher in Ecclesiastes. The shackles of envy, resentment, anger and futility that come from seeking earthly pleasures can all be cast aside when we receive the promises of Jesus.

Through his death on the cross, Jesus offers us hope and purpose. He knows what we need to survive and flourish in this life, and he promises us a future where pain and suffering are banished and there is freedom, justice, joy and peace – a deep, enduring contentment. If we're struggling with ill health, grief, abuse or shattered dreams, we can take comfort from the fact that this world isn't all there is.

I was challenged recently reading a book by the television presenter Sian Williams. Her brother-in-law had been given a diagnosis of terminal illness, but instead of asking, 'Why me?', he resolved to say, 'Okay, there's no cure for this so what can I do during a tricky time to make life more bearable, more enjoyable?'

Instead of dwelling on what we don't have or what we'd like to be different, we can consider the things we're grateful for and gain comfort from them. We may be blessed with the love of family, a job, a home or generous friends who listen. Or it could be relief from pain, a good night's sleep, a bed for the night or leaves on the trees.

The American television presenter and philanthropist Oprah Winfrey says, 'Be thankful for what you have; you'll end up having more. If you concentrate on what you don't have, you will never, ever have enough.'

Begin a gratitude diary, noting down all the things for which you're thankful. And if things are tough, remember the power and purpose we have through Christ.

CATHERINE LARNER

True satisfaction

Then Jesus declared, 'I am the bread of life. Whoever who comes to me will never go hungry, and whoever believes in me will never be thirsty.' (NIV)

Whatever our personal circumstances, it's easy to take these words literally. If times are hard, then we want to know Jesus will provide. If life is comfortable, then we might approach Jesus with a shopping list of requests for making things even better.

While Jesus does want the best for us, he is asking us to have a different perspective. Instead of focusing on all that this world may have to offer, he wants us to set our eyes on eternity and our relationship with him. It is possible, then, to know contentment in this world through our confidence in being with him forever.

He's offering us so much, yet we're easily distracted. We're sold the lie of the world that we shouldn't suffer or go without. It can make it hard for us to hold on to the bigger picture.

However, when things are taken away, we often realise what brings us true and lasting happiness. I know for myself, when I'm enjoying life, my focus slips. It's easy to become complacent and I can lose my passion in prayer.

When things are tough, I look more intently on God's word and pray with eagerness and expectation of hearing him speak. I long for the comfort and peace only he can provide and earnestly seek what God might be teaching me.

The theologian Henri Nouwen said: 'I have found it very important in my own life to try to let go of my wishes and instead to live in hope... when I choose to let go of my sometimes petty and superficial wishes and trust that my life is precious and meaningful in the eyes of God, something really new, something beyond my own expectations, begins to happen to me.'

Two questions to consider: am I pursuing contentment through health, wealth and happiness in this world? What does it mean to me that Jesus can and will give me eternal life?

CATHERINE LARNER

Love of money

Keep your lives free from the love of money and be content with what you have, because God has said, 'Never will I leave you, never will I forsake you.' (NIV)

Packing a bag for a trip away always focuses the mind. What do I really need? How can I keep things to a minimum? Our world becomes both smaller and larger as we open ourselves to a new experience.

I have enjoyed camping in recent years. It's been the most refreshing and liberating experience. It hasn't been wild, cold or wet, I have to say, but there's something about following the rhythm of the day, going to sleep when it's dark, taking time to prepare and eat meals and only having the essentials with you.

Every time I return home I am grateful for the comforts of walls, a bed and hot water, but it makes me aware of how little I really need to be content. I've found it important and useful to have this regular self-evaluation because the more things in life we accumulate, the less they seem to bring us satisfaction and the more we want.

At the peak of his wealth, the business magnate John D. Rockefeller was worth about one per cent of the entire US economy. Yet when asked how much money was enough, he answered, 'Just a little bit more'.

God doesn't deny us the good things in this world, but we are urged to remember that we shouldn't seek meaning and purpose from money, status or possessions, because these things are transitory. No matter what wealth or achievements we accumulate, ultimately this life comes to an end. Inner peace and joy only come from our faith and trust in God.

If we feel that possessions have got a hold of us, we should get rid of them. Contentment comes from holding everything lightly as we fix our eyes on what remains when everything else has gone.

Why not try to get rid of one possession each day for the next week? Donate it to charity or recycle it. You will feel a sense of release and relief in getting rid of the burden of having too many possessions.

CATHERINE LARNER

Becoming Christlike

'Blessed are the poor in spirit, for theirs is the kingdom of heaven.'
(NIV)

It's tough to learn that we can find true happiness by living a life which seems to offer the opposite. Poverty, sorrow, persecution, humility, meekness – who would want to experience these things rather than a warm home, plenty of food, clothes and security?

However, instead of striving, achieving and possessing the things of this world and ultimately still finding ourselves to be empty, we are urged to seek fulfilment spiritually. In these few short verses from the sermon on the mount, Jesus outlines how we can become more like him. We are called to live like Christ and to allow Christ to live through us. Being one with God through Christ is our ultimate aim. But we have to change our understanding of the world completely to live this life.

And it's quite an undertaking. Even when we take the eight verses one by one, some of these qualities are harder for us to embrace than others. How easy is it to be humble, to turn the other cheek, to show forgiveness or to be insulted?

If we begin in a small way, in the everyday, we can train ourselves to find contentment in all we do. The 17th-century monk Brother Lawrence 'practised the presence of God' in the ordinary tasks of life. He never complained about the menial jobs he was required to do in the monastery. Instead, as he washed up, cleaned the floors or prepared the food, he used the time as worship. As Brother Lawrence himself said: 'Is it not quicker and easier just to do our common business wholly for the love of him?'

Read the verses from the sermon on the mount, stopping to contemplate each quality Jesus wants us to pursue. Close your eyes and ask God to tell you how he wants you to adopt that quality in your life today.

CATHERINE LARNER

Pressing on

Not that I have already obtained all this, or have already arrived at my goal, but I press on to take hold of that for which Christ Jesus took hold of me. (NIV)

For most of the world, contentment has negative associations. It is seen as accepting, settling and being satisfied, complacent even.

Work appraisals encourage us to think about what we can do better, how we can achieve more, where we see ourselves in five years' time. We're expected to have ambition, to seek promotion, to want more money, more stuff, more status.

For Paul, contentment isn't a passive concept and our goal is something entirely different. Instead of seeking achievements for our place in the world, Paul believes the most contented follower of Christ is pressing on to know him better and deeper, to be more like him.

Contentment is about looking away from ourselves, from our needs and desires and, instead, seeing God and reflecting his glory. Contentment is about putting Christ first. It is a constant yearning to see God's kingdom come and his values be upheld now and forever more.

It means putting the past behind us. This may mean claiming God's forgiveness or it may be a case of setting aside regret, sadness or bitterness. It is acknowledging what is now most important – our relationship with Christ and pushing forward for that.

Contentment, then, is something we need to acknowledge and reach for, and it is something that we can learn to gain.

If we seek God's glory rather than our own happiness, then we will experience contentment. God wants us to enjoy him. We won't glorify God by being satisfied, but we can be satisfied in God.

Pray with the psalmist: 'I will praise you, Lord my God, with all my heart; I will glorify your name forever' (Psalm 86:12).

CATHERINE LARNER

Learning

I know what it is to be in need, and I know what it is to have plenty.
I have learned the secret of being content in any and every situation.
(NIV, italics mine)

Here it is! The secret of contentment.

Paul is writing to the church in Philippi when his life is once again under threat. Christians are being thrown to the lions and being burnt alive, yet his letter is one of joy and encouragement. He has experienced illness, and he's been beaten, shipwrecked, imprisoned and persecuted. But he has also known success and prosperity, so he is qualified to tell us how to live in any circumstances.

There is no checklist, though. We tend to look around us for things that will make us content, but Paul says we need to put the effort into learning how to be content. It takes willingness and effort.

Contentment is a choice. And as such it is something we pursue. We aren't born with it, and we don't wait for God to bestow it on us; instead we achieve it through surrendering to Christ. It is in him the secret of contentment lies. We cannot find this contentment in our own strength, but as Paul says: 'I can do all this through him who gives me strength' (v. 13).

Contentment is an ongoing process, it doesn't happen overnight. If we think about how we learn a musical instrument or a new language, or even how to drive a car, it takes time, perseverance and commitment. We need discipline to adopt a regular habit, to keep going when it gets hard.

I've been trying to learn Italian and while there are elements of it I love, I mostly find it tough. The test is how much we keep going when the task doesn't come easily. If we are motivated, if we have our eyes on the goal, that helps. So, if we keep our eyes on Jesus and focus on getting to know him better and finding out what he wants for us in the circumstances in which we find ourselves, then this will keep us going and help us towards contentment.

Any time you are challenged during the day, hold out your hands and recite Philippians 4:13. Whatever you're facing, gain strength from Christ – there is contentment in him.

CATHERINE LARNER

Choosing our attitude

**I know what it is to be in need, and I know what it is to have plenty.
I have learned the secret of being content *in any and every situation*.
(NIV, italics mine)**

Paul knew that contentment lay not in his external situation, but in his heart, mind and soul. It came from his relationship with Christ. But how do we cope with the challenges of daily life? Paul tells us it can be done, but while we can count our blessings if life is comfortable, what if we're suffering abuse or loss, injustice or illness? We know that Christians will experience hardship and persecution for their faith. How are we prepared for this?

I am reminded of Corrie ten Boom's account of her time in the Ravensbrück concentration camp, recounted in *The Hiding Place* (Chosen Books, 1971). She and her sister endured horrific conditions in their dormitory, yet Betsie prayed, 'Thank you for the fleas.' Corrie exclaimed, 'This was too much. "Betsie, there's no way even God can make me grateful for a flea."' Her sister reminded her that we are urged to give thanks in all circumstances. Later, the sisters realised that those fleas meant that the guards kept well away from their dormitory, where together they were able to read and pray.

Sometimes in the moment we can't appreciate how God is working, but by trusting in him we can be content in the harshest situation.

Another Holocaust survivor, Victor Frankl, wrote in his book *Man's Search for Meaning* (English translation first pubilshed by Beacon Press, 1959): 'When we are no longer able to change a situation, we are challenged to change ourselves… The last of human freedoms is the ability to choose our attitude in a given set of circumstances.'

Contentment can bring us peace and comfort. If we are unable to change our situation, what good does it do us to fret and worry? Trust in the Lord. Hope in the midst of suffering is where we may find contentment.

Lord, thank you for all that you have given me in my life today. Help me to praise you for the things I enjoy and to look for you in the things I find challenging. Amen

CATHERINE LARNER

15

Leaning in to God

For Christ's sake, I delight in weaknesses, in insults, in hardships, in persecutions, in difficulties. For when I am weak, then I am strong. (NIV)

There is no pecking order of tragedy. One life isn't harder or easier than another. We all have our issues to deal with, and it is pointless to compare our lives for blessings or woes.

We don't always understand why we go through suffering, but we can often make sense of it afterwards. Weakness and brokenness are often where we meet God more clearly. I know in my own life that when everything is stripped away, and I can no longer rely on myself or others, I have leaned most heavily on the Lord.

If we are open to God's love and healing, we can learn from difficulties. God works both in and through our circumstances. Having confidence in him, that he is in control and will work things for good, brings us a peace and contentment.

In her book *Broken Works Best* (Monarch Books, 2012), Catherine Campbell describes how two of her three children were born disabled with a life-limiting disease and died aged 10 and 13. She says that through this time of terrible sadness and trials, she experienced tremendous peace. 'It was pain that sent me to his word on more occasions than joy, enabling me to learn more about the wonderful character and plans of God.'

A friend told me that when she had been going through difficult times, she was given a picture of a tent peg. She was being knocked really hard, but each blow was driving her closer to Jesus, making her stronger and more resilient.

As Madeleine L'Engle wrote in *The Summer of the Great-Grandmother* (Farrar, Straus and Giroux, 1974): 'It's a good thing to have all the props pulled from under us occasionally – it gives us some sense of what is rock under our feet and what is sand.'

Try not to go to bed dwelling on anything negative that may have happened today. Instead, think of something positive, then that memory will be cemented in your mind. When facing adversity, learn, grow, accept.

CATHERINE LARNER

Waiting

Each person should remain in the situation they were in when God called them. (NIV)

We've forgotten how to wait. These days we expect everything at the touch of a button. We write an email and expect an answer within the hour. Photographs are available immediately rather than having to get them developed. Even many television series are available to watch in one sitting rather than over a number of weeks. We think we can't be at peace until we have what we want, until it has come to fruition.

Waiting for the answers to prayer is even more difficult, then. We can become focused on receiving the answer instead of seeing how God is working in our lives now, in the waiting.

It is good to have hope for the future, for better things, particularly if life now is tough, but that shouldn't be our purpose. We don't know what is in store and we shouldn't squander what we have now for some bigger hope which may never materialise.

There are many examples in the Bible of individuals who had to wait – Abraham and Sarah for a son, given to them in old age; Moses in the desert before God called him to free the Israelites from captivity; Paul's ministry seemingly hampered by illness, persecution and imprisonment. But their waiting wasn't passive, it was active.

Henri Nouwen says that we perceive waiting as holding on for something outside of our control: waiting for the bus, for an operation, for a reply. But 'if we wait in the conviction that a seed has been planted and something has already begun, it changes the way we wait... It is giving up control over our future and letting God define our life.'

Heavenly Father, forgive me for my fears for the future, my impatience at being at this place and for questioning the story you've written for me. Help me to trust that I am safely held by you. Amen

CATHERINE LARNER

A new attitude

Do not conform to the pattern of this world, but be transformed by the renewing of your mind. (NIV)

It's easy to get sucked into the ways of the world. Work colleagues or parents at the school gates remind us every day of the latest big thing – the most desirable holiday destinations, the decisions over new kitchens, new cars or new houses. Or there might be details of a tragedy – a bereavement, a terrifying diagnosis, job losses or money difficulties – that leave us shaking our heads, grateful we're not going through the same things ourselves. We tend to compare our lives with others, and not just our neighbours or colleagues, but sometimes television personalities or people in the news.

Whether we feel envy or superiority, neither is a good outlook, but these are the consequences of pitting our circumstances against one another, being distracted from where we are in our relationship with Christ. We aren't owed anything in this life. We shouldn't expect things to go the way we want them. Society tells us it should be the case, but that only brings disappointment.

I have a strong, attractive and confident friend who loves nice things, has a comfortable home, comes from a good and extensive family and who has great stories to tell about her past exciting and high-profile career.

I also have a friend who struggles to manage her money, grieves over a difficult relationship with her late mother, mourns being single and without children and had to take an administrative job beneath her capability because of a breakdown.

You might have guessed it – they are the same person. I viewed her as successful and happy, but she presents a front to hide her sadness and dissatisfaction.

It's a question of perspective. The danger of comparing our life with others is that we see only what we want to see. Very often our thoughts destroy our contentment. Here in Romans, we are called to renew our minds – and transformation, freedom and contentment will follow!

Think about how you view your life, its joys and its disappointments. How might others see you? What does God see? What talents and gifts has he given you? How is God working in your life? What blessings do you enjoy?

CATHERINE LARNER

God's purpose

And we know that in all things God works for the good of those who love him. (NIV)

How many times have we heard this verse spoken to us when times are hard? Sometimes it is helpful, but other times it's very hard to accept, believe and trust in.

I know of women who have miscarried much-wanted children. One spent her life eaten up with regret and longing for what would have been her third child, resentful of her husband for not wanting them to try again. The other mourned her loss but delighted in the child she had and relished the family they were together.

Some people believe that because of their tragedy, they are unable to live their best life. But if we go on living a life of regret, we can't find contentment with where we are now. You can't spend your life thinking about what might have been. And though we have experienced a loss or a disappointment, why do we think we have been robbed or deprived? God may have been protecting us from some greater tragedy.

American poet and civil activist Maya Angelou said: 'You may encounter many defeats, but you must not be defeated. In fact, it may be necessary to encounter the defeats so you can know who you are, what you can rise from, how you can still come out of it.'

We mustn't be imprisoned by past failures and mistakes, nor must we squander the present with our dreams for the future. To look to the world for purpose is fruitless. It is only God who brings meaning to our lives.

A failed relationship, a miscarriage, a disabled child, singleness – there are many times in life when things haven't worked out as we would have hoped. How do we deal with that disappointment?

Imagine yourself at a point in your life when things suddenly changed for you, when you wish things had happened differently. Imagine Jesus there alongside you. Talk to him about how you feel and allow him to speak to you.
CATHERINE LARNER

All we need

'Love the Lord your God with all your heart and with all your soul and with all your mind.' (NIV)

It's easy to dismiss some people's qualities or attitudes to life as being due to their personality and therefore unattainable for the rest of us. But we've seen how contentment isn't something we're born with. Instead, it is something we can cultivate and nurture. And the rewards are great. Contentment makes us happier and healthier.

I have a friend who I believe has learned to be content. There is a quiet surety about her and a simplicity in her approach to life. She hasn't been afraid to go against the expectations of society in terms of her career progression and material possessions. She has a quiet wisdom and a sense of justice. Most of all she trusts and puts her faith in God. She spends time with him – praying, reading and listening – and she has a passion and a delight in being in his presence. The result is a deep peace, a contentment and an expectation that God will provide all that she needs. It is something very attractive.

We might feel we've failed God if we aren't happy and smiling each day. But contentment is something different. It's being confident in our faith, our identity, our hope and our future. It isn't found in trying to change our circumstances, but in serving God in whatever circumstances we're in. It is about what is on the inside not the outside. Other people might control the world around us, but only we can control the world within us.

Contentment brings a soul-satisfying relationship with God. Christ will always be enough.

Seek to practise contentment: want what you have and be thankful; don't make comparisons, but focus on your God-given talents and gifts and accept your imperfections. God loves us as we are.

CATHERINE LARNER

Using the armour of God (Ephesians 6)

Di Archer writes:

One of our children's favourite praise songs had the words, 'You've got to put your armour on, you've got to put your armour on, so you'll be safe!' (Ernie and Debbie Rettino, 1990). Our children loved the concept and gladly sang along. It was a bouncy, upbeat song which still plays in my head now – for me, it is inextricably linked with the verses we are about to consider together. But it also contained a serious message. In his letter to the Ephesians, Paul is saying that we who follow Jesus cannot avoid the fact that we face opposition. Aligning ourselves with the Lord means that we are not just part of his family, but also part of his army. Putting our trust and our lives into the hands of our loving Lord Jesus, and going his way, means that we are choosing *not* to go other ways. And some of the battles and difficulties we face very often feel like someone, or something, is against us. In addition, one look at the news confirms that many of the world's troubles seem instigated and sustained by malign forces – they are hard to explain in any other way.

Being enlisted into an army was probably not uppermost in your mind when you became a Christian. But you are part of it, nevertheless. Whether it is a fight to overcome a destructive behaviour that is ruining your life, a fight for peace in your local Christian community that seems so at odds with itself or a fight against a systemic social evil, there are battles to be won.

You may not feel like a fighter, and some of us may struggle to relate to the military language and imagery. On a bad day it can be hard to put a toe out of bed, let alone put on the armour of God that Paul recommends. On days when I seem to be fighting myself, rather than any useful kingdom battles, I try to remember that I am not alone – we are all in this together. And after all, I am a beloved daughter of the king of kings, not superwoman!

The good news is that God has provided what we need to fight well. Learning how to use his provision takes time and practice. The best way to learn is together, so why not share these daily reflections with a fellow soldier and invite someone to join forces with you for this week?

The battle is real

A final word: Be strong in the Lord and in his mighty power... For we are not fighting against flesh-and-blood enemies, but against evil rulers and authorities of the unseen world, against mighty powers in this dark world, and against evil spirits in the heavenly places. (NLT)

As a 'final word' in a letter to a church, this takes some beating. The apostle Paul has inspired and challenged his listeners throughout his letter and ends with this clarion call to stand firm in God. Coming hard on the heels of a culture-changing list of how we are to treat each other, which must have caused a good deal of reaction (chapters 5 and 6), Paul does not let us off the hook.

Paul wants us to focus on two things. First, he wants us to remember that the battles we face are not against other people as such, but against the spiritual forces behind everything, from disconcerting mischief-making to serious relationship troubles, to national discord and war. While sometimes we must challenge other human beings, we must always recognise that there are larger powers at work. When we want to blame or slap someone (or am I the only one who feels like doing that?), it might help to cool our temper by bearing this in mind. It might restrain us from actions that we later regret. It also helps to explain the rampant misery in the world that too often threatens to beat a path to our door.

How do we cope with the reality of malign opposition? The answer is Paul's second focus – to 'be strong in the Lord and in his mighty power'. Such easy words to say and yet they contain a whole world of perspective. Will we choose to stick close to Jesus no matter what? When our pain screams so loudly that we cannot hear his voice? When we feel abandoned? When the bad things look like they are winning? It may be 'fingernail faith' at these times but seek your strength from the Lord who is always with you.

Read John 16:33. Jesus has it more in hand than we can imagine.

DI ARCHER

How it's done

Therefore, put on every piece of God's armour so you will be able to resist the enemy in the time of evil. Then after the battle you will still be standing firm. Stand your ground, putting on the belt of truth…
(NLT)

It is said of Susanna Wesley that despite having 19 children, she spent time with God daily by sitting in her favourite chair and throwing her apron over her head to give herself space to pray. She homeschooled her children, both boys and girls, in classical and biblical learning, ran a 200-strong Bible study group and survived her minister husband's frequent absences. Two of her sons, John and Charles, grew up to change the Christian world, founding the Methodist Church and bequeathing us thousands of hymns.

Extraordinary stuff. Susanna faced and met her challenges well. She knew how to both wear and use the armour of God. Her confidence in the mighty power of the Lord is fabulous. Perhaps you know fellow believers like that. Maybe you are one – someone like Judge Deborah, who took God at his word and set off into battle, trailing dependent men in her wake (Judges 4:7–9).

These women do not go into a fight unprepared. How do we copy their example and 'resist the enemy', so that we too can stand firm? First, by putting on the belt of truth. Presumably Paul was thinking of a Roman soldier's armour here. The belt was essential for holding your underclothing in place, for the scabbard to hang on and as a base for the rest of the armour. It held you tight at your core.

Isn't this what we need? To know deep in our heart that the truth of God holds us steady. To rely on his faithfulness, his presence and his good purposes towards us. To be defined by his radical love for us. To have peace, deep inside, because of God's kindness in saving us. What is one truth that you need to help you resist the enemy and stand firm, with or without an apron?

Thank you, God, for your unending faithfulness to us. Thank you that your love never wavers. Help us to depend on it. Amen. (Read Isaiah 49:15–16).
                                                          DI ARCHER

Treasuring your heart

Put on the full armour of God, so that… you may be able to stand your ground… Stand firm then, with the belt of truth buckled around your waist, with the breastplate of righteousness in place… (NIV)

If Paul thought that putting on the armour of God was necessary in order to stand firm against the strategies of the devil, then, like it or not, we would do well to take it seriously. What helps you to relate to this? I have done various things over the years: sometimes thinking of the pieces of armour while I am getting dressed in the morning, sometimes counting my 'Morning, God! I am busy today, please help' as that vital connection with my heavenly Father which arms me for the day. Roman armour doesn't look all that attractive and might feel removed from 21st-century life – that doesn't really matter of course, but it does help to visualise putting it on. Imagine it protecting you and giving you what you need for the day ahead.

The second piece of armour is 'God's righteousness'. It's the breastplate, protecting your heart from attack. It's Jesus rescuing you from sin and fear, and making you his child. It's the power to live in the freedom and security of that. It's the invitation to follow in Jesus' footsteps, living in honesty and righteousness yourself so that you don't give the devil a foothold. You don't need to fight for your place in the world – it is already assured. You don't need to put others down in order to feel better about yourself – you are loved and accepted just as you are. You can trust that you are always held and always seen. You have been made right in every way that matters.

The devil would have you believe otherwise. He would want to undermine your confidence and worth. But your heart is covered by his righteoussness, it is precious to God – so stand firm.

Dear Father God, thank you that you know my heart. Please may you guard it today. Amen

DI ARCHER

Don't be slipshod

For shoes, put on the peace that comes from the good news so that you will be fully prepared. (NLT)

The important thing about the footwear that Roman soldiers wore was its durability. It was one of the main reasons why the Roman army swept to victory in so many countries – they had the best boots. Other armies were badly equipped in comparison; Roman boots just kept going, protecting their wearers from all weathers, keeping their feet healthy and supporting them in long marches across the continent. Made from layers of leather, heavy-soled and hobnailed with iron, they gripped well and endured for the long haul.

So that's why we need them too. First, of course, because we need that peace of the good news for ourselves. It is so easy to lose in this demanding, noisy, challenging, ever-changing world. But we need to step out into it with the right shoes on – that inner reassurance that God is with us every step of the way.

Second, this peace is not just for us but also for us to give away. This is another reason why we need brilliant boots that give us a really firm footing, not only to keep our balance, but also to go forward and take ground for God's kingdom. We take Jesus' presence with us everywhere we go, just by having our boots on. We have prepared ourselves and are ready to tell our God story wherever we can. Imagine yourself walking with his peace around you, in all your familiar places. He is with you, he is with you, here and there and everywhere you go.

The good news of peace is durable. It protects you, keeps you healthy and supports you. It gives you the best grip so you can go out into the world with confidence that you are on the winning side.

Plot spoiler: we really do have the victory. Have a look at Revelation 1:12–18.
                                                                      DI ARCHER

Armour really works

In addition to all this, take up the shield of faith, with which you can extinguish all the flaming arrows of the evil one. (NIV)

When Roman legionaries put on their armour, a servant passed them each part in turn. Piece by piece they readied for battle. But they had help.

As, of course, do we. We are not alone. Like King David in the Old Testament, we have a first-class trainer: 'He trains my hands for battle' (Psalm 18:34). For King David, it was a physical battle; for us it is usually other fights. However, whether our battle is moral, emotional, spiritual, physical or something else, we are not solo soldiers.

Take the shield of faith. The Roman shield was fashioned from light wood and leather, held together by metal and soaked in water to put out the flaming arrows of the enemy. It was large, rectangular and covered the soldier down to his knees. You've probably seen pictures of how legionaries locked them together in front and above their ranks to provide an impenetrable box of protection. Thus, dressed well in their brilliant boots, they could advance, together.

We are left with two obvious lessons: one, shields are absolutely no use unless we use them; and two, they work better when we work together. So, every time we pray the Lord's Prayer, when we ask God to 'deliver us from evil', pick up your shield. You are on God's side and the battle is his. Ask him for help with your current challenges, especially if you are feeling hard-pressed and 'under attack'. Stand firm and resist the undermining thoughts, fears and worries. Choose to find things to give thanks for. Hold up your shield. And if it's hard to lift, ask others for help. Ask a friend to pray for you. Keep yourself in Christian community. It works.

The devil is the father of lies (John 8:44). What truths do you need to proclaim to extinguish his flaming deceit?

DI ARCHER

Oh, happy day!

Put on salvation as your helmet.(NLT)

Have you ever seen what a Roman helmet looked like? Sure, it was made of solid bronze, with pieces extending to protect the cheeks, nose and back of the neck – all vital in a physical battle. But any soldier of rank also had a crest or plume of red dyed horsehair on the top. Imagine how intimidating it would have been to have a sea of strong red coming at you. It wasn't just for show, however. For Romans, red was the colour and symbol of Mars, their god of war. In their mythology, it identified them as a warlike people, descended from this god.

So when we put on our helmet of salvation, we are saying similar things. We are identifying ourselves as belonging to someone and something – to a person and purpose. We are declaring that we belong to Jesus, that we are obedient to his lead, that we are part of his army of followers and that we are dependent on him for provision and direction. We are also trusting that he will protect us from the worst of knocks on the head. Or at least provide a hospital tent for recovery and healing.

Given that our position in the ranks is secure because we are saved by Jesus Christ, what is our equivalent of the bright red plume? How does the world know that we are Christians? What are the characteristics that we display? How can we 'take ground' for the kingdom of God? Unlike the god of the Romans, we have a Spirit who brings love, joy, peace, patience, kindness, goodness, faithfulness, gentleness and self-control. How can we spread these further, both within and around us?

Smile – you belong to Jesus. No matter what you are facing, he is with you. He will be faithful. Read Genesis 39:21.

DI ARCHER

Swing to win

Take the sword of the Spirit, which is the word of God. Pray in the Spirit at all times and on every occasion. Stay alert and be persistent in your prayers for all believers everywhere. (NLT)

During an extremely stressful time in my life, when our daughter was struggling with a severe eating disorder, I bought a wooden sword from an historic castle shop and used it in my agonised praying for our girl. It really helped to chop and swing as I prayed and shouted for deliverance. It reminded me that Paul didn't just fling down a few jolly words about the armour of God as an interesting illustration to bring his letter to a close. He wrote about armour because he knew we needed it.

I really don't like being in a battle. But I know that it is real, and when I remember to don my armour, it goes so much better. And if Jesus needed the word of God as his sword to defeat the father of lies, then so do I. Jesus fought the devil toe-to-toe with God's truth in the desert in a way we will never have to. The devil promised him authority over kingdoms in exchange for worship and Jesus responded, 'The Scriptures say, "You must worship the Lord your God and serve only him"' (Luke 4:8). The devil finally conceded because he lost his footing. Jesus took all the ground. During our eating disorder days, I clung to God's word for dear life. Thankfully, our daughter came through and the charity tastelife (**tastelifeuk.org**) was born in response to help others.

The battle is always about truth. It starts in our hearts and heads. It is seen in our actions. It is often bitter and frequently feels impossible. It lands us flat on our faces too many times. But God will meet us even there, in all the mess and pain. The message is always, 'Do not be afraid' (Isaiah 41:10).

'Be the kind of woman that when your feet hit the floor each morning, the devil says, "Oh no… She's up!"' (Joanne Clancy).

DI ARCHER

God's view of work

Amy Boucher Pye writes:

I've always loved work. Perhaps it's partly the influence of my parents, both of whom grew up on farms and who never shy away from getting their hands dirty and getting something done. Maybe it's partly how I'm wired. But I love producing and working and creating – even to the point of my mother once saying, 'You know you don't have to do *everything* all at once.' Or a former boss saying that I 'eat work'.

I don't say this in a reverse-compliment way – look at me, look at me, I produce so very much. Downsides of this particular trait are that I sometimes put projects over people or I work until I drop with exhaustion or even illness. I need to embrace a healthier – indeed, a biblical – view of work.

And so, writing these notes came at a good time. Ironically, I was worn out from, yes, too much work and even sought out a fellow writer friend to take over this commission. I felt spurred on from God to relinquish this project and was content when she said yes. But circumstances interfered, and when the project came back to me, I smiled wryly at God. 'Okay, Lord; can you rescue me again? I promise to rejig my life.'

Work, as we'll see in our first reading, came before sin entered the world. That is, God has always had it as part of his plan for women and men to flourish. But after Adam and Eve disobeyed, the curse of the fall affected our work. And now we often face office politics, drudgery, feeling unseen, menial tasks and so much more – whether in paid employment, the voluntary sector or homemaking.

But the good news is that God is in the business of redemption. He always seeks to bring his kingdom here on earth, and he entrusts us to collaborate with him in this grand task. We can work and enjoy it; we can create good things by the work of our hands or of our minds.

I hope, whatever your particular situation, that you'll come away from this fortnight re-energised and reinvigorated when it comes to your work. How exciting to think of the effect on the world when we collaborate with God!

Redeeming work

The Lord God took the man and put him in the garden of Eden to work it and take care of it. (NIV)

Sometimes I want to rub my hands together in glee: I get *paid* to explore the Bible and share what I'm learning with others?! Okay, so the payment may not be massive, but the privilege is great. Sometimes when I'm writing Bible reading notes or doing research, I lose all sense of time in the wonder of the project. Not always, of course! My work, like yours, has its aspects of drudgery and pain.

But this sense of joy relates to something vital about work that I pointed to in the introduction – it's part of God's good plan for humanity. Note in Genesis how God made Adam, placed him in the garden of Eden and immediately set him off to work, instructing him to care for this place of paradise. Work comes before Adam and Eve disobey God, which brings about many negative consequences. God designed his people to create, shepherd, oversee and build.

Imagine what work would be like if our first parents hadn't ignored God's instructions. Each of us would know what we're put on the earth to do and would love every minute of doing those things. Alas, that's not the world we live in, but through God's Spirit, we can get glimpses of this reality. God wants us to usher in his kingdom, and how we spend our energy and focus is – amazingly – part of his plan of redemption.

Why not spend some time with God, asking him to show you a time when you felt truly alive when doing work (and of course I'm including voluntary and unpaid projects and tasks as part of that definition)? What do you notice about common threads in what surfaces for you? How could you pursue more work of this kind?

Loving God, thank you that you've created me in your image and have given me the ability to work. Help me to know where to put my focus and energy, that I might bring you glory. Amen

AMY BOUCHER PYE

God sees

From heaven the Lord looks down and sees all mankind; from his dwelling-place he watches all who live on earth – he who forms the hearts of all, who considers everything they do. (NIV)

Recently I was discussing the subject of disability theology with my friend and fellow writer Tanya Marlow, who shared her insights and wisdom. We were talking about work, and she mentioned her severely disabled friend Jenny, whose list of physical challenges shocks and saddens me. They include a devastating complication from surgery that has profoundly affected her neck. Tanya observed, 'Jenny works all day simply holding her head up.'

What does work mean when we aren't able to produce in the sense that the world expects? We know that God sees us and he's the one who ultimately defines what it means to work. So many people work and contribute to society in ways that are countercultural – such as without payment and often not being noticed for what they give to their community. People such as Jenny, whose heroic daily efforts simply to continue living inspire me. God sees and knows: 'From heaven the Lord looks down and… watches all who live on earth' (vv. 13–14). He who formed the hearts of his people 'considers everything they do' (v. 15). His eyes are on us; in him and his 'unfailing love' we put our hope (v. 18) because 'he is our help and our shield' (v. 20).

In the west we've been so conditioned to equate people with their projects and accomplishments. As you ponder how God has made us to work, consider what working means in our culture and how you think God's view might differ. Is there a disconnect between the two? How does that shape how you live and act? Where might you need to shift your views?

May we be those who value all of the people God has created and formed.

Loving Lord, you've made me in your image. Help me to collaborate with you, in whatever form that means and within whatever limitations I face. Thank you for seeing and loving me. Amen

AMY BOUCHER PYE

Fearing God

You will eat the fruit of your labour; blessings and prosperity will be yours. (NIV)

The 'fear of the Lord' seems to have gone out of favour these days; instead, we tend to emphasise friendship and intimacy with God. I'm all for that, but I've experienced the benefits of fearing the Lord too.

What do I mean by this phrase? It's common in the Old Testament – perhaps the most well-known verse is 'The fear of the Lord is the beginning of wisdom' (Proverbs 9:10). When we fear God, we're acknowledging that he is God and we are not. He is mighty, all-powerful, all-knowing, the creator, our maker. We honour and serve him and want to bring him glory. And thus we fear him – not so much a sense of terror, as the word can often entail, but rather a holy sense of awe and wonder.

Psalm 128 employs this sense of the fear of the Lord as it gives a blessing on those who revere God. And those who fear God will reap the bounty and blessings of the work of their hands – they will 'eat the fruit of [their] labour' and 'blessing and prosperity' will be theirs (v. 2). The idea here is an agricultural worker enjoying the harvest with their family, feasting around a table. The vine in verse 3 is often used in the Old Testament to denote God's people; here it symbolises a wife who brings her husband blessing and richness.

An exercise to foster a healthy fear of the Lord is to take some time and prayerfully list some of the names and attributes of God. The more we name – such as creator, redeemer, Lord, God Most High – the more we are lifted out of ourselves and up into transforming worship of the one true God.

'The fear of the Lord is the beginning of knowledge, but fools despise wisdom and instruction' (Proverbs 1:7).

AMY BOUCHER PYE

Clearing the rubbish

Put your outdoor work in order and get your fields ready; after that, build your house. (NIV)

As I write, my kitchen is slowly being transformed. As I mentioned, I've been overly busy during the past months and one effect has been on the state of our home. I'd be far too embarrassed to have you round for tea; not only are there piles of stuff threatening to topple over, but you'd also notice the built-up grime. After some false starts, we've found someone to help me bring order to our vicarage, and grateful I am.

As I read these sayings from King Solomon, therefore, I resonated with them in a not-so-wonderful way as I considered the sluggard with his thorns, weeds and ruined stone wall (vv. 30–31). I realised that I needed to heed the wisdom of Solomon and attend to all areas of my life.

Solomon asked God for 'a discerning heart' (1 Kings 3:9) and God answered generously, making him the wisest of men. Here he's instructing future leaders in how to live wisely and well. An important part of flourishing is planning: 'Put your outdoor work in order and get your fields ready; after that, build your house' (v. 27). Only after we clear the fields and prepare the ground for the foundation should we build a house. And Solomon warned against an outlook of putting things off to tomorrow, as he warned against 'a little sleep, a little slumber…' (v. 33).

After some intense cleaning or clearing of fields, we can more easily stay on top of our homes or gardens. We can apply the same principle to our spiritual lives. Is there any clearing out of rubbish that we might need to do in our relationship with God or with others, so that we can more easily maintain a clean and healthy partnership?

Loving God, you want me to flourish. Give me your wisdom to do so. Help me to put into practice what I'm learning that I might better love you and others. Amen

AMY BOUCHER PYE

Chasing after the wind

Yet when I surveyed all that my hands had done and what I had toiled to achieve, everything was meaningless, a chasing after the wind; nothing was gained under the sun. (NIV)

Do you ever feel like you're spinning your wheels? You set plans in place for a project, but you meet resistance or stumbling blocks along the way. Unexpected challenges crop up that mean what you've planned for no longer applies. You sigh in disgust, throwing up your hands, wanting to give up.

The book of Ecclesiastes has that flavour. Traditionally the author has been seen as King Solomon, but scholars debate whether or not it was him, especially because a style of writing known as 'pessimism literature' in the ancient Near East grew out of his wisdom writings (this book very much fits into that genre!). We can feel confused over why Ecclesiastes is in the Bible, with its conclusion that everything is meaningless (v. 11).

But what we need to consider is that this book shows us what life is like without an eternal perspective – it's folly and foolishness. The writer plumbs the depth of human pursuits and finds them wanting. Having great things – homes and vineyards, gardens and parks, fields and herds – all in the end mean nothing without God.

When we've invested a lot of time, energy and perhaps money into a project, we might be tempted to infuse its results with more meaning than we should. Instead, we can leave the impact to God. Thus, for me as an author, I do my best in writing and launching a book, but whether it sells very well or very poorly I can leave the judgements to God.

How might you adopt an eternal outlook in the work you're doing? Whether you're based in your home or in a Christian or secular arena, we can do our best and trust God for the outcomes.

Lord, if what I've set my hand to is useless and meaningless, please redirect me. Help me to partner with you in my pursuits, that they may make a difference eternally. Amen

AMY BOUCHER PYE

Jesus' yoke

'Come to me, all you who are weary and burdened, and I will give you rest. Take my yoke upon you and learn from me, for I am gentle and humble in heart, and you will find rest for your souls.' (NIV)

Launching two books while keeping up with my other deadlines has been a joy and a challenge. I feel like I'm now nearing the end of a marathon and hitting the wall. The finish line is coming into view, but I'm not sure if that makes the going easier or harder. Part of me just longs to have reached that point where I can switch off and rest.

We all long for rest, not least because after the fall of humanity our work entails drudgery and toil. Quite simply, it wears us out. But Jesus looks at us lovingly, extending his arms and inviting us to come to him to find rest (v. 28). One Bible commentator, referring to the King James Version, says that the phrase 'ye who labour' implies the burdens we take upon ourselves, while 'heavy laden' points to the burdens we've received from others. Either way, we need the rest that Jesus gives.

Note in this passage Jesus' gentleness and humility. He reminds us that he's not a taskmaster who expects results from us – or even that we produce anything at all. Rather he calls us to take upon ourselves his yoke, which is easy, and his burden, which is light (v. 30).

What would this look like for you in your current situation? Perhaps you agreed to some projects some time ago that now feel heavy. Could you find someone to take one or more of them on – after all, they might be excited! Or maybe there's something you're itching to do but you've lacked the confidence. How could partnering with Jesus – knowing that you're yoked to him – help you to take the first step in pursuing a new venture?

May we find rest for our souls in Jesus.

Loving Lord, you know me; you know what excites me and what exhausts me. Keep helping me know myself better, that I would learn to say 'yes' and 'no' to the things that will help me to flourish. Amen

AMY BOUCHER PYE

One thing needed

'Martha, Martha,' the Lord answered, 'you are worried and upset about many things, but few things are needed – or indeed only one. Mary has chosen what is better, and it will not be taken away from her.' (NIV)

I wouldn't say I'm house proud – living with my family has enabled me to tolerate much more mess than I could previously. But when our family hosts people for a meal or to stay the night, I do have certain standards. The floor needs to be vacuumed. The loos cleaned. The top layer of dust really does need to be removed. Oh, and providing something homemade for breakfast is good too.

Thus, I don't think you'll be surprised to hear that I have a soft spot for Martha. Here she is, bearing the brunt of unexpected guests, while Mary sits at Jesus' feet. No wonder Martha gets all het up. The unfairness! The burdens! The lamb that needs cooking and the table that needs to be laid! Doesn't Jesus realise that this meal won't come together on its own?

But Jesus, speaking lovingly to Martha, says that Mary has 'chosen what is better' (v. 42). He's not telling Martha that work isn't important, but rather that Mary has honed in on the one thing that matters instead of being distracted by many other good things. Maybe Martha needs to chill out a bit – like I often do when hosting guests – and focus on the people more than the trappings of hospitality. I imagine Jesus would have been happy with leftovers and dusty floors.

Martha's home in Bethany was Jesus' second home, where he could come to relax. He longed to relate to Martha as a person rather than merely enjoying her finest cuisine. Jesus loved her and wanted her to be relieved of the burdens she'd taken on herself. He points her to a better way of living. One that I – and maybe you – need to embrace.

Lord Jesus, you love us so much that you don't want us to be stuck in unhelpful patterns of living. Show me if I'm focusing on things that don't matter. If so, help me redirect my attention to you. Amen

AMY BOUCHER PYE

Empowering God

In his defence Jesus said to them, 'My Father is always at his work to this very day, and I too am working.' For this reason they tried all the more to kill him. (NIV)

One of my favourite themes in the Bible to ponder is the indwelling of Jesus in those who believe in him, and the loving relationship between the members of the Trinity – the Father, Son and Holy Spirit. How God dwells in us through his Spirit, and how Jesus and the Father and the Spirit are one, affects everything – including work.

In today's passage, when Jesus speaks about his relationship with his Father, the Jewish leaders are so incensed that they try to kill him (v. 18). Why? Because Jesus calls God 'My Father', an attribution the Jewish people wouldn't make. They would instead say, for instance, 'My Father in heaven', to reflect the distance between them and the holy God. In calling God his Father, Jesus makes 'himself equal with God' (v. 18).

But because Jesus and the Father are one, Jesus only does 'what he sees his Father doing' (v. 19). The Father gives him authority to carry on his work on the earth. And they don't limit their work to themselves – God invites us to participate in it through the Spirit who dwells within us, as we see later in John's gospel. There Jesus speaks about how he empowers his followers to do the work of him and his Father: 'Believe me when I say that I am in the Father and the Father is in me; or at least believe on the evidence of the works themselves. Very truly I tell you, whoever believes in me will do the works I have been doing' (John 14:11–12).

This, then, is the work we are called and empowered to do. Because of the mystery of God's Spirit living in us, we can collaborate with God to usher in his kingdom here and now.

Triune God, fill me with your presence, that I might overflow with your love and light. Empower me to work for your glory. Amen

AMY BOUCHER PYE

True work

Then they asked him, 'What must we do to do the works God requires?' Jesus answered, 'The work of God is this: to believe in the one he has sent.' (NIV)

A week ago, we were thinking about disability theology and what it means to work when personal limitations apply. Today's story from John's gospel seems to shed some light on the question. Here's what had been happening – great crowds came to learn from Jesus, and he'd fed the throngs with the boy's two fish and five loaves (see John 6:1–13). More crowds then gathered later, eager to see what Jesus would do next. When they found him, he named what was really going on within them, that they were looking for him because they'd eaten 'the loaves and had [their] fill' (v. 26). Jesus went on, 'Do not work for food that spoils, but for food that endures to eternal life' (v. 27).

This food that will not grow mouldy is the work we're called to do – to believe in Jesus. In one sense, that's it. Whether we're incapacitated, fully fit or somewhere in between, we're called to 'believe in the one he has sent' (v. 29) – then we can 'do the works God requires' (v. 28).

I love the freedom in Jesus' answer – that the work God calls us to do is simply to believe. All of what follows will flow out of this one main emphasis, according to our individual personalities, preferences, hindrances and limits. This work is the 'one thing necessary' that Mary chose, as we saw on Saturday.

How could keeping in mind this definition of work change the way you approach the tasks in your day? Keeping this question in mind could form a good basis of a quiet day or a retreat, as we ponder how we best respond.

Lord Jesus, I believe in you. Your Father sent you to earth to usher in his kingdom. As the risen Christ, you live and reign. Help me to honour you. Amen
AMY BOUCHER PYE

Hearts to respond

One of those listening was a woman from the city of Thyatira named Lydia, a dealer in purple cloth. She was a worshipper of God. The Lord opened her heart to respond to Paul's message. (NIV)

Did you realise that the first convert to the Christian faith in Europe was a woman? I don't think I did until I read it in a Bible commentary. Lydia was a businesswoman too, a dealer in expensive and luxurious cloth – for purple in the ancient Near East would have been rare and valuable.

Note the process of her conversion. Her physical location reveals that she was seeking after the things of God – she was by the river, where Paul and his team, including Luke, expected 'to find a place of prayer' (v. 13). She was already a worshipper of God when she heard the message, and 'the Lord opened her heart to respond' (v. 14). Isn't that beautiful? We see the partnership between a person's desire and God's loving response, giving her the faith to believe.

Note too that she was a persuasive person. After she and her family are baptised, she convinces Paul and his people to come and stay at her house. I imagine she must have peppered Paul with questions about how to live as a follower of Jesus. I'd love to have sat and observed that gathering!

She may have supplied her cloth to the most important dignitaries, but her most important work was what we saw yesterday – to believe in the Lord Jesus. Her home became a centre of mutual encouragement and trust, and the base for Paul, Silas and others.

You might think I'm banging on about the same message, day after day. You might be right in that! Perhaps we need to hear more than once that our work is to believe in Jesus. That's enough.

Loving God, you spurred on Lydia to believe in you; you took her openness and desire to know you and multiplied it. Please do the same in my heart and in my life. Amen

AMY BOUCHER PYE

Something useful

Anyone who has been stealing must steal no longer, but must work, doing something useful with their own hands, that they may have something to share with those in need. (NIV)

The apostle Paul embraced a huge task in teaching and discipling those in the new churches that sprang up as a result of his missionary travels. It seems that many – or at least a distracting few – were not doing the 'one thing necessary' in following Jesus wholeheartedly. And so Paul wrote to the churches with instruction, encouragement and sometimes hard words of correction.

In his missive to the Ephesians, he spends the first half exalting God for how he's freed us by his grace. In the second part he focuses on the change that comes when we embrace the new self instead of being mired in the activities of the old self. He explains how we should live as those who believe in and follow Jesus.

Related to our theme of work, notice how Paul centres on those who have been stealing and how, in order to counter this, they must have something productive to put their hands to. Instead of taking from others, they must work so that they can give to others. What a difference that would make to their conception of who they are! No longer thieves but generous givers who show their love for others practically. As Paul had said to the Ephesian leaders as he left them, knowing he'd never see them again on this earth, 'It is more blessed to give than to receive' (Acts 20:35). This truth informed his instructions for those who were stealing.

When you consider your work (however that's defined) during a set period of time such as the last month or year, how have you found focusing on the 'one thing necessary' while also pursuing good and fruitful work for your hands?

'So whether you eat or drink or whatever you do, do it all for the glory of God' (1 Corinthians 10:31).

AMY BOUCHER PYE

Antidotes to busybodies

'The one who is unwilling to work shall not eat.' We hear that some among you are idle and disruptive. They are not busy; they are busybodies. Such people we command and urge in the Lord Jesus Christ to settle down and earn the food they eat. (NIV)

A busybody in church. What comes to mind when you read that phrase? Why do I guess that the image that comes to mind is of someone from your current – or perhaps former – body of believers who makes it their business to 'helpfully' point out the failings and imperfections of the church leadership (or others)? And I guess that perhaps you can bring to mind more than one such person?

Paul doesn't mince his words to the Thessalonians. He tires of those who are 'idle and disruptive', naming the truth of their behaviour: 'They are not busy; they are busybodies' (v. 11). In contrast, he points to his and his team's behaviour as a model, how they have worked 'night and day, labouring and toiling' so as not to be a burden (v. 8). In strong words he commands and urges them 'to settle down and earn the food they eat' (v. 12). As for those who aren't busybodies, they should never grow weary in 'doing what is good' (v. 13).

When we come up against busybodies in church, we might be tempted to share what we think of their activities and how they make us feel. Perhaps instead we could prayerfully consider how we might work with them creatively. Could we invite them to contribute to a project we're part of? After all, they may be feeling left out and overlooked, with their criticism coming from a place of pain.

But we must also exercise discernment. Paul warns the Thessalonians not to associate with those who are truly busybodies. We therefore need God's help in working out the best way to proceed, and we can trust that God won't fail us.

Lord, let me not take the speck out of my neighbour's eye if I have a log lodged in my own. Show me if I'm acting like a busybody, whether in my church or community. Amen

AMY BOUCHER PYE

41

Love in action

Faith by itself, if it is not accompanied by action, is dead. But someone will say, 'You have faith; I have deeds.' Show me your faith without deeds, and I will show you my faith by my deeds. (NIV)

Scholars have differed over the years, but most agree that the James who wrote the New Testament letter is the half-brother of Jesus, son of Joseph. As the introduction to James in the *NIV Bible Speaks Today* (IVP, 2020), which I highly recommend, observes, the letter reads like a sermon by one of the beloved leaders of the church that has been taken down in written form. James led the church in Jerusalem, so he'd fit this style.

He speaks with love, but also without holding back, as he calls those who follow Christ to develop and mature in their faith. Indeed, he points out that faith cannot be separated from actions: 'Suppose a brother or a sister is without clothes and daily food. If one of you says to them, "Go in peace; keep warm and well fed," but does nothing about their physical needs, what good is it?' (vv. 15–16). He continues, saying that faith without deeds is dead.

James continues in making his case, naming as examples two characters in the Old Testament: Abraham, who was lauded for his faith, and Rahab, who was praised even though her profession would have made her unclean. Both put their faith to the test as they acted in courageous ways that could have disrupted their lives. James then calls his fellow followers of Jesus to combine their faith and deeds.

We don't need to be working for a church to put our faith into action. Whether something as simple as holding the door for a vulnerable person or sending a message to someone to encourage them, we can show God's love in a myriad of ways.

'Whatever you do, work at it with all your heart, as working for the Lord, not for human masters, since you know that you will receive an inheritance from the Lord as a reward' (Colossians 3:23–24).

AMY BOUCHER PYE

Serving God forever

'My reward is with me, and I will give to each person according to what they have done… Blessed are those who wash their robes, that they may have the right to the tree of life and may go through the gates into the city.' (NIV)

When the angel takes him on a tour of the new heaven and the new earth, John takes in a glorious sight. No more tears or crying or pain, because the new order has been put into place (Revelation 21:4). It's a life that we cannot now fully conceive, for 'no longer will there be any curse' (22:3).

Note the second half of verse 3, which we may easily skip over in the wonder of what follows with their being no night because of God being the light: 'The throne of God and of the Lamb will be in the city, and his servants will serve him.' With God they 'will reign forever and ever' (v. 5).

That's our glorious commission for eternity – to serve God and reign with him in a city where there's no death or dying or tears, no night or pain or betrayal, no heartache or lies. God doesn't show John – or John doesn't share if he did – what it means to serve God and reign with him. But if the surroundings are anything to go by, we won't be bored. Our work will be the most fulfilling and fruitful that we've ever undertaken, and I'm guessing that we'll suffer no repetitive strain injuries, burnout or other ailments.

Take heart, friend, in your work. As we've seen over this fortnight, we don't have to produce anything to work for God and bring him glory. Our main work is to believe in Jesus, putting our trust in him. When we do that, we'll be empowered by the indwelling Spirit to exercise our creativity as we seek to marry our faith with our actions.

Glorious God and the Father of our Lord Jesus Christ, I long to be with you in that new city. Strengthen me in my life and work while I wait in joyful hope for your coming again. Come, Lord Jesus. Amen

AMY BOUCHER PYE

People like us
(1 Corinthians)

Sheila Jacobs writes:

When I think about the Corinthian church, I imagine it was a bit of a mess.

All sorts of things were going on. Why else would the apostle Paul need to write a long letter to the Corinthians – one of two, in fact – giving them plenty of advice and even stern rebuke? But as I have been writing these notes, I've had to smile. I'm not sure the church today is any different to the church all those years ago. That's why this letter is so relevant.

It was written with passion, love and grace. Paul loved these people, even if they clearly exasperated him at times. Doesn't that make Paul, and the Corinthian believers, all the more real? The Corinthians were stumbling around getting it wrong, but they were still God's children. They needed help – some good, sound teaching from someone who loved God and who loved them and wanted to encourage them to live well for Jesus. Surely we could all benefit from that kind of mentor! Chapter 15 in particular is truly inspirational; think how encouraged the Corinthians would have been to read Paul's uplifting words about the resurrection!

The Corinthians were immature, quarrelled often and were prideful. Paul had to discuss with them issues of unity, sexual morality and more. And yet God showered his gifts upon them, just as he is willing to do today. The famous chapter on love (1 Corinthians 13), placed so neatly between chapters dealing with spiritual giftings, is a welcome reminder that whatever we do, however we worship, whatever our theology, there needs to be an attitude of love and respect for all God's people. In fact, that is what I came away from these notes thinking: love and respect, stemming from the grace of God, is what it means to be a member of the body of Christ.

I have followed the book pretty much chapter by chapter here, and while you may not have time to read the whole of 1 Corinthians, I do encourage you to read the passages suggested. They're pertinent, challenging and helpful. Of course, if you do have the time, making a study of the whole of this book would be very worthwhile.

As you read, I pray you may find something that personally speaks to you or into a situation that you find yourself in.

May you grow and be blessed as we look at 1 Corinthians together!

No striving!

You are in Christ Jesus, who has become for us wisdom from God – that is, our righteousness, holiness and redemption. (NIV)

When I first became a Christian, I was thrilled that Jesus was real. It was amazing. It was like life had exploded into full colour. Jesus was alive and he loved me. What a difference that made! Everything seemed to make sense. Where I'd been struggling, I knew he would help me. He cared. I could know him! I wasn't alone anymore.

It was a whole new world, being lived at a different level, with new opportunities. I just wanted to work for God, to tell people about him, to do stuff… work, work, work!

But then I got ill. I couldn't do anything at all, for God or for anyone else. Terrible dizzy spells would suddenly hit me. I couldn't keep my job; I could barely walk down the path.

At this time, someone sent me a book. It was *Sit, Walk, Stand* by Watchman Nee (CLC Publications, 2009). It explained how we needed to rest before we could do anything for God. It is from a place of rest that we can then walk as he wants us to walk and stand against anything that comes against us.

I realised for the first time what 'grace' really meant. Jesus is my wisdom from God. He himself is my righteousness. He is my holiness. He is my redemption.

I have no righteousness of my own. No holiness. It's all his.

Once that really began to sink in, it altered my way of thinking. I could rest, knowing I would move more as I trusted in what he had already done in me and what he would do. I had to let go. In truth, I could do little else, I was so poorly.

But that lesson has stayed with me these many years. No need to strive!

I have no righteousness of my own. Jesus is my righteousness! He himself is my holiness. My redemption. How does that thought inspire you to respond? Take some time to reflect, think about it and pray.

SHEILA JACOBS

God's power

My message and my preaching were not with wise and persuasive words, but with a demonstration of the Spirit's power, so that your faith might not rest on human wisdom, but on God's power. (NIV)

Paul admits here that when he speaks, he isn't relying on his own strength, skill and ability, but on 'a demonstration of the Spirit's power' (v. 4). Why? So that his hearers won't put their faith in him, but in God!

When I was exploring faith, I read a book written by a woman who had a powerful testimony. That story changed my life. I suddenly understood that it was possible to know Jesus personally, something I hadn't realised before. God really spoke to me, just as I'm sure he has spoken to you on many occasions through the words of others, whether written or spoken.

Some people are gifted communicators. There are speakers who spend a long time preparing a methodical sermon; others have a more relaxed approach. Whatever the style, whatever the gifting, we have to look beyond those things, beyond those people, to God himself – what he is saying and doing, and how he is endorsing what is being shared. We 'have the mind of Christ' (v. 16), which means that, through the Spirit living in us, we should be able to discern what is of God – and what is not.

When the Spirit comes, people's lives are changed. Sometimes the power of God brings healing and miracles – or it can manifest in a word of knowledge or prophecy. Hebrews 4:12 tells us: 'For the word of God is alive and active' – a word from God, directly for us, from the heart of the Father can be utterly life-changing.

Whether we experience a physical, mental or emotional touch from God, our faith should always be in him, not in his servants. Paul was relying totally on the power of the Spirit. Do we?

Lord, help my faith to always rest on you and not on human wisdom. Thank you, Jesus, for your power in my life and in this world. Amen

SHEILA JACOBS

Divisions

You are still worldly. For since there is jealousy and quarrelling among you, are you not worldly? Are you not acting like mere humans? (NIV)

The early chapters of 1 Corinthians are exciting. In chapters 1 and 2 we read of the wisdom and power of God. But in chapter 3, Paul has some serious problems to address.

It seems there were divisions within the Corinthian church. People were siding with different leaders. 'I follow him.' 'Really? Well, I follow *him*.' Sound familiar? 'I really liked our last pastor, but this one… well, not so much.' 'I don't agree, our new minister is brilliant. I've learned so much from her.'

Paul sounds a little exasperated here. 'It doesn't matter *whose* preaching and teaching you prefer. Just don't get into arguments, don't get jealous,' he says. 'We're all in it together.'

And we are. The church is God's temple (v. 16), being built together brick by brick, person by person. We 'together are that temple' (v. 17).

Jesus told his disciples that the way people would know they were his followers was if they loved each other (John 13:35). People won't come to know God because we prefer someone's teaching to someone else's. They will come to know him if we love each other and let that love flow out to a watching world that needs Jesus so desperately.

As we fix our eyes on Jesus, and follow him more and more wholeheartedly, then we'll avoid petty disputes and quarrelling that cause divisions. These are just distractions. Yes, we respect those who teach, lead and help lay the foundation stones of our faith. But ultimately, we need to live to please our Master and to obey him. We are of Christ, and he is of God (v. 23). We may not always agree with each other, but let's not let that stop us going forward together in love, just as he has called us to do.

Imagine the members of your church as living stones (1 Peter 2:5), being built together as God's temple. How does this challenge your perception of fellowship? How might it encourage you to think differently about church?

SHEILA JACOBS

Follow my leader

This, then, is how you ought to regard us: as servants of Christ and as those entrusted with the mysteries God has revealed. Now it is required that those who have been given a trust must prove faithful. (NIV)

It isn't easy being in leadership. Whether it is church ministry, in secular employment or in a voluntary capacity, it's a big responsibility.

In the first book of Corinthians, we can see how much Paul cares for the people he's writing to. He is their spiritual father and is concerned for their growth, and he urges them to imitate him (vv. 15–16).

People look up to leaders. They learn from them. This could cause those in leadership to have an inflated idea of their own importance. But Paul isn't speaking arrogantly here. He explains that those who are given the responsibility of leadership, of teaching, of revealing the ways of God to those who are learning, have been given 'a trust' (v. 2) and therefore faithfulness is required. The leader is a servant under God, and Paul says that he doesn't much care how others judge him; he is judged only by the Lord (v. 4).

If we are in a position of leadership, especially if we are caring for God's own people, then we are servant leaders, just as Jesus was. Servants of the Lord, leading and caring for those he loves. If we remember that, it will keep us humble.

Perhaps today you are feeling the weight of leadership, knowing that people are looking to you, depending on you. The only way to lead well is to rely fully on God and to refresh and replenish ourselves by spending time daily with him. We need to hear from him, to understand what he is saying to us and to the people under our care. It's about spending time in that secret place, so that when we come out from his presence, we will be confident in *his* strength and not our own abilities.

Are you in a position of leadership? How much time do you spend with Jesus each day? Be careful not to let the responsibilities drown out your precious time with him.

SHEILA JACOBS

Choices

You must not associate with anyone who claims to be a brother or sister but is sexually immoral or greedy, an idolater or slanderer, a drunkard or swindler. Do not even eat with such people. (NIV)

This is a challenging passage. The Corinthian church was well-known for its lack of moral standing. In chapter 5, Paul is addressing a particular problem of sexual immorality. In chapter 6, he then goes on to talk about lawsuits. It's all about living 'right', living well before the Lord and being different from the world.

Believers in Christ are meant to 'live different', but it isn't easy when we live in a culture that is so very different from the kingdom of God. We may look at the way people live today and shake our heads, even condemn them. But Paul says we need to concentrate on how *we're* living, not point a finger at a world that does not know Christ.

We need to live different to show how real Jesus is, as well as to honour him. As we spend time with Jesus, we will get to know him better and we will learn what pleases him. And that will mean our lives should look very different to the lives of people who don't yet follow him.

1 Corinthians 5:9–11 makes for sober reading. In effect, Paul is drawing a line. Christians are free to associate with people who don't live Christ's way and don't claim to – how else will unbelievers ever get to know him unless they see him living in and through us? Instead, Paul is talking about believers ('claims to be a brother or sister', v. 11) and how we need to keep our lives clean. If someone says they're a Christian but their life is not honouring God, perhaps they need a gentle reminder of whose they are and just what that means.

We all make mistakes; we all get it wrong. But as we mature in Christ, we need to make consistent lifestyle choices that honour God.

If you know someone who claims to be a Christian and yet is living a life that is clearly not pleasing to God, pray for them now. How is your own lifestyle shaping up?

SHEILA JACOBS

Single or married

An unmarried woman or virgin is concerned about the Lord's affairs: her aim is to be devoted to the Lord in both body and spirit. (NIV)

When I read 1 Corinthians 7 as a young Christian, it spoke to me powerfully. Marriage is great. But *it's okay to be single*. Although the context here is of a 'present crisis' (v. 26) and Paul clearly expected the Lord to return soon, it's a passage that has encouraged me greatly throughout the years.

Sometimes the Lord calls us to be single for a season. This single season – however long or short – can be a time of preparation, of waiting; an opportunity to get to know Jesus better, without distraction. But sometimes God may ask people to be single, full stop.

What! To give up *everything* for you, Jesus? All my hopes and dreams? A family, even? Are you asking me to trust you even with this? That can be a daunting prospect. Yet I – and perhaps you too – know of lifelong single people who seem perfectly content with their situation. They fix their eyes on Jesus and grow closer to him, without the distractions of partner and family.

Maybe, though, you know that's not your calling. You might be waiting for the right man to come along. Perhaps he's taking his time. Tempting, isn't it, to look outside of God's people for a partner?

In verses 7–9 of this chapter, Paul tells us that both marriage and singleness are gifts of God. Different people are gifted with different things. He knows the destiny he has for us, the plans that he has for our individual lives (Jeremiah 29:11). We are not our own, we're his; we were 'bought at a price' (1 Corinthians 6:20).

God knows our desires. Whether he is gifting us with marriage or with singleness, our focus must be on Jesus. He knows what path he has chosen for us. Can we trust him with that?

Lord, I trust you with my life. You have a good plan for me. I commit my future to you. I choose you first. I'm your disciple and I want to follow you, whatever my life circumstances. Amen

SHEILA JACOBS

Focus!

Do you not know that in a race all the runners run, but only one gets the prize? Run in such a way as to get the prize. (NIV)

I'm not a great one for sport, but I admire the dogged determination and discipline of athletes. They compete against others, but really they are competing against themselves.

As we follow Jesus, we're not in competition with other people, but Paul here is employing a useful metaphor as he describes the Christian life. It's like a race. Keep your eyes on the prize. Focus! Don't get sidetracked.

It's easy to take our eyes off the finishing post, isn't it? There are so many interesting distractions along the way, things that delight the eyes and make us forget, perhaps temporarily, that we are running the race for God. Paul talks about athletes' 'strict training' (v. 25) to enable them to win an earthly prize. How much more should we take our race seriously, if we are aiming for a heavenly crown?

Nothing is worth losing our precious crown – the reward that awaits us when this life is over. Life on this earth is short. But something far better awaits us. Whatever entertains us here, whatever excites us and thrills us, is nothing compared to the riches of Christ which are eternal.

In this world, we sometimes walk with him through difficult circumstances, and at times we can lose heart, become discouraged, even disappointed with our life journey. One thing runners don't do is look back. That is pointless and can cause them to lose the race.

We might regret choices we've made or chances we've lost. But today, let's remember we're in that race: the race that ends somewhere beautiful. We can't change yesterday, and while memories can be wonderful, we shouldn't live in the past. Not when a future crown awaits us!

Are you distracted? Are the things of this world causing you to lose your focus? Do you live in the past? What can you do today, and in the days ahead, that will help keep you focused on Jesus?

SHEILA JACOBS

Freedom!

'I have the right to do anything,' you say – but not everything is beneficial. 'I have the right to do anything' – but not everything is constructive. (NIV)

We're free! We don't have to do anything to get right with God, except believe in his Son and receive the salvation he offers. Jesus died for us, removing anything that separates us from God – taking away our old nature and offering us a new, clean life in him. He rose from the dead, proving that his words were true. So we can be free of our old ways of living: ways that did not please God. That's grace. God's free, unmerited, unearned favour.

So, I can do anything I want now, right? Can I get away with anything because God will just forgive me?

It is true that he will forgive when we repent – turn away from our wrongdoings – but the grace and freedom we have in Christ doesn't mean we are free to do anything we like at any time. Grace means we are profoundly grateful to God, and we want to please him. Pleasing him means choosing his way, which may not always agree with our own desires!

It can be a constant battle not to go our own way, especially if God seems to be taking his time when we've asked him for something. But going our own way can be destructive. We can choose to run ahead of God and finish up in a situation which, as Paul points out in today's passage, is not beneficial or constructive.

So, what does freedom really mean? Is it freedom to do what we like – or freedom to do what we know to be right? Take a look at 1 Corinthians 8, which talks about being careful regarding how we use our freedom in case we compromise the conscience of others.

We're free. But how will that freedom impact our daily choices? What does freedom in God mean to you?

Lord, thank you for the freedom you purchased for me on the cross. Thank you that I can be free to fulfil the plans you have for me. Help me to use my freedom well. Amen

SHEILA JACOBS

The Lord's Supper

The Lord Jesus… took bread, and when he had given thanks, he broke it and said, 'This is my body, which is for you… This cup is the new covenant in my blood; do this, whenever you drink it, in remembrance of me.' (NIV)

I sometimes take Communion on my own or with a friend. It can be on the phone or on Zoom! At those times, I tend to read these verses from 1 Corinthians. Jesus told us that the bread symbolised his broken body; the cup and the wine, the shedding of his blood. This is the new covenant between God and humanity. We take part in the Lord's Supper to remember Jesus and what he did for us.

Verse 26 is interesting, because it tells us that when we do this, we 'proclaim the Lord's death until he comes'. It's an important and serious occasion; that's why we need to 'examine' ourselves (v. 28) before we share Communion.

What does it mean, to examine ourselves? I think it's about reflecting on the attitudes of our heart, being real before God, and saying sorry or asking God to forgive us and help us in our present circumstances. We shouldn't treat the Lord's table with any kind of disrespect, because we are remembering what he did when he died an agonising death for you and for me. God's favour, his grace, costs us nothing – it's free – but, of course, grace cost Jesus his life.

Among the celebration and the worship and the excitement of remembering whose we are, let's remember how amazing it is that we have friendship with God and eternal life. It's an adventure. It's deep and real. But if it wasn't for Jesus, we'd still be far from God.

Thank God for Jesus and for what he has done for us. Thank God that he was obedient, even to death (Philippians 2:8).

When we take the bread and wine, let's do so with reverence and humility as well as joy!

Perhaps you would like to take Communion alone or with a friend. Or the next time you take it in church, remember with special gratitude what Jesus has done out of his love for you.

SHEILA JACOBS

Spiritual gifts

God has placed the parts in the body, every one of them, just as he wanted them to be. If they were all one part, where would the body be? As it is, there are many parts, but one body. (NIV)

This is a great chapter, all about spiritual gifts – which are different from the spiritual fruit (see Galatians 5:22–23). Spiritual gifts are distributed by the Holy Spirit (vv. 4, 11), the 'same Lord' and 'same God' (vv. 5–6) at work in the differing forms of service.

Looking at the various gifts, perhaps you can see which ones God has chosen to give to you – and which ones you'd love to have. They are all useful for building up both other people and ourselves. Some may find God gives them special wisdom for another person or for a certain situation; or a word of knowledge – knowing something that could not naturally be known – for the edification of someone else. Others may discover they are prophetic, able to hear from God and encourage people through a word, a picture or a dream. Some may speak in languages they have never learned, praying God's words or praising him, when known language doesn't seem to be quite enough.

How good God is that he gifts us individually and as a body of believers, so we can all work together, helping, supporting and blessing one another.

Of course, it might be easy for us to become puffed up with pride. But we have to remember these things are *gifts*; we haven't earned them. And each person is different; we need to respect others' giftings.

We all need each other and each other's gifts. Let's encourage one another to find out more about what God has given to us and what he wants to give. Perhaps it is time to start asking God to reveal the gifts he wants to bless us with and ask him to show us if anything is blocking the flow of those gifts.

Jesus, thank you for all you have given me and all you want to give. Help me to be open to whatever gifts you want to give me today, so I can please you and bless others. Amen

SHEILA JACOBS

That love chapter!

Love is patient, love is kind. It does not envy, it does not boast, it is not proud. It does not dishonour others, it is not self-seeking, it is not easily angered, it keeps no record of wrongs… It always protects, always trusts, always hopes, always perseveres. (NIV)

Even if you're not a regular churchgoer, you've probably heard these words before – at a marriage ceremony, perhaps. They can be summed up as 'Love never fails', as we read in verse 8.

It's a famous chapter, nestled in between chapters 12 and 14, which are about spiritual gifts. There can be plenty of division within the church about the nature of gifts, and perhaps that's why this little piece on love is placed here. Whatever we think about spiritual gifts, and the nature of them, let's always remember to walk in love.

When I look at this passage, I am challenged about how loving I really am. Am I easily angered? Do I keep a record of other people's wrongdoings? Love makes it easier to forgive, but love can also make us vulnerable.

People let us down. Sometimes they mean to, sometimes they don't. I let people down too. I am far from perfect. Sad to say, the kind of love seen in this chapter is not always evident in me.

However, I am reminded that God himself is love (1 John 4:8). Try putting his name in there: 'God is patient, God is kind. God is not easily angered, and he keeps no record of wrongs. God always protects, hopes, perseveres.' How does that affect our view of God? And what does it mean that God loves *me* that way and that much?

When we think of 'love', we can often be bombarded with images of romantic 'stuff' – hearts and flowers, candles and pretty cards. Maybe you experienced some of these things yesterday, Valentine's Day. Maybe you didn't. But the most precious love of all is God's own love for you and for me. His love never fails.

Thank you, Jesus, for your great love for me. Please fill me with your Holy Spirit, so that he may be visible to the person in front of me, who really needs to know your love. Amen

SHEILA JACOBS

Order, order!

For God is not a God of disorder but of peace – as in all the congregations of the Lord's people. (NIV)

Reading through chapter 14 of 1 Corinthians, we can see how Paul instructs the church to respect each other during times of meeting and worship. It's a supernatural gathering, after all, and gifts are evident. But that doesn't mean people are weirdly out of control (v. 32). Things need to be done properly, and here Paul teaches the church how to behave!

I don't know what your church is like – you may come from a charismatic background or one that is quieter and more traditional. But either way, there needs to be room for God to break in when he chooses to do so and to break out to change people's lives.

God equips his people in different ways, as we have already seen in these notes. But it is apparent here that while Paul expects spiritual gifts to be in operation, there is no need for disorder.

Of course, we can't put God in a box. He is sovereign. He might choose to do something that astounds us. Something we haven't thought of. Something that doesn't fit our theology! But there's no room for chaos. God is a God of peace, as Paul tells us in verse 33.

Maybe we have seen things that have rather put us off the more charismatic experiences. But reading through this chapter slowly, perhaps we can see, with Paul, how it's meant to be. We have a supernatural God so we can expect supernatural events to occur, in and through his children. Still, we must be discerning – what's of God and what's not? We need to ask God for wisdom. But let's make sure any negative experiences we may have had don't hinder us from being blessed and built up by the gifts he wants to bring.

Lord, thank you that because I am your child, I can expect 'God things' in my life, things that will amaze and encourage me. May your name be glorified in all things, Lord, God of peace and power. Amen

SHEILA JACOBS

The hope of life

When the perishable has been clothed with the imperishable, and the mortal with immortality, then the saying that is written will come true: 'Death has been swallowed up in victory.' (NIV)

At the time of writing, I am grieving the loss of a friend. It's so sad to think that this person is no longer there for me to text, to say hello to. There will be no Christmas card this year. There's zero chance now of a random meeting. They will play no part in my future, although they were significant in my past. Death is so silent, so final. Or is it?

With Jesus, of course, there is hope. In 1 Corinthians 15, Paul talks about the resurrection of the dead, and it is well worth reading this whole chapter if you have the time. There is so much encouragement here. Our bodies are not meant to last forever. They are temporary structures. We can't imagine now what it will be like once our physical bodies have fulfilled their earthly function, but this chapter is rich in imagery around what it will be like once the old has been put aside and the new has come.

If we know Christ and are trusting in him, we know that our bodies, which are perishing daily, will one day be swallowed up by death – but after that, something 'imperishable' will come (v. 53). Death itself will be 'swallowed up in victory' (v. 54)!

While sin puts us in the grave, grace allows us to transcend it. No wonder Paul encourages us to give ourselves 'fully to the work of the Lord' (v. 58), sharing this good news with people who don't yet know him – the good news that Jesus is alive, that he loves us and he offers us eternity with him. The 'dead end' doesn't have to mean it's all over. There's real hope in Christ's victory – in the gift of eternal life.

Is there anyone you can offer the hope of life to today? Can you share the good news of what Jesus has done with a friend, a neighbour or a relative? Ask God about it now.

SHEILA JACOBS

It's personal

I, Paul, write this greeting in my own hand… The grace of the Lord Jesus be with you. My love to all of you in Christ Jesus. (NIV)

The end of this letter to the often-troubled Corinthians is all about love. Paul has had some strong words to say to them, but he clearly loves these people.

Sometimes we have to say things that we know will challenge others. But, like Paul, let's be gracious and loving about it.

This first letter to the Corinthian church is full of love and grace. I like the way Paul finishes here; he's written these closing words himself. He has sent greetings to the Corinthians from other believers (vv. 19–21). It's as if he is crying out: 'Look, you belong to Jesus. So – follow him! We all love you. We're rooting for you. So just love each other.'

I think this is a big message for the church today. We might worship in different ways – my style might not be your chosen style. We may have points of theology on which we don't always agree. But if you love Jesus, then you're my sister or my brother!

Psalm 133 tells us how God blesses us when we live in unity. Jesus himself said that it is as we love each other that people will see that we are his (John 13:35). Paul is teaching the same thing. Our own personal preferences, our own viewpoints, whatever gifts we possess – let's not let anything get in the way of love.

As we look to Jesus and receive his Spirit, as we surrender ourselves to him, then we will start to truly walk in a way that honours and reveals him. He is love, and he wants to show his love to the people who don't yet know him.

And of course, he wants to show his love to me and to you. It's personal!

How has Paul's first letter to the Corinthians helped you? Challenged you? Encouraged you? If you keep a journal, jot down some important points. How might the message of 1 Corinthians influence your faith journey today?

SHEILA JACOBS

Walking the wilderness with God

Rachel Turner writes:

Many people in the Bible spent time in the wilderness. Moses led the Israelites through 40 years of living in the wilderness to get to the promised land. Hagar was driven into it when she was forced to leave Abraham's household. David hid in the wilderness when King Saul was trying to kill him. John the Baptist lived and preached in the wilderness, and it was in the wilderness where Jesus was tempted by Satan.

What comes to your mind when you read the word 'wilderness' in the Bible? I instantly conjure images in my mind of a vast, barren, dry landscape, where heat radiates off a sea of dirt and rocks and a harsh, hot wind whips dry plants and sparse trees. It seems to me to be a place of loneliness, dryness and want, where mere existence is hard. The wilderness is not a place I want to be.

Yet, many of us will experience a sense of living in a 'wilderness' – a season of loneliness or dryness. A season of feeling out of our depth or overwhelmed at the harshness of our situation. The wilderness is not comfortable or comforting. You may have lived through wilderness seasons or you might be in one now.

Naturally, we want to do everything we can to survive the wilderness and get out quickly. To us, it is a place to be avoided at all costs.

But God seems to view the wilderness differently. He describes Israel's time in the wilderness in surprising terms, 'I remember the devotion of your youth, how as a bride you loved me and followed me through the wilderness, through a land not sown' (Jeremiah 2:2, NIV). God described the 40 years the Israelites spent in the wilderness like a honeymoon – a beautiful time of connection, of learning how to walk together and build a joint life for the future.

While we see the wilderness as a harsh and painful place, God can turn it into a beautiful season of life with him. Scripture is brutally honest about the experience of the wilderness. It allows us to hold the tension of both truths: the reality of the struggle of wilderness seasons and the existence of God's good character within it.

Over the next two weeks, we will explore together the beauty and power of walking the wilderness with God.

When

'When you pass through the waters, I will be with you; and when you pass through the rivers, they will not sweep over you. When you walk through the fire, you will not be burned; the flames will not set you ablaze.' (NIV)

Something inside of us longs for the easy, perfect path – the garden of Eden experience, the VIP package. We want life to be simple, fair, beautiful and struggle-free. God does promise that one day we will have that: an eternity with him when 'he will wipe every tear from their eyes, and there will be no more death or sorrow or crying or pain' (Revelation 21:4, NLT).

But that is not now. We currently live in a broken world, full of sin and complication. God's promise is not that he will give perfect lives on earth to people who love him. He promises that he will be with us when it isn't perfect.

In today's passage, we see one word repeated again and again. The word 'when'. Not 'if', but 'when'. *When* bad things happen, then *this* is what God will do. Jesus told his followers, 'In this world you will have trouble…' (John 16:33). We Christians are not being set up for a perfect, carefree life just because we love God and he loves us.

Instead, we are being encouraged to encounter a God who will see us through the wilderness, not prevent us from ever entering it. So much of God's promises are on the other side of 'when': his provision, his presence, his protection, guidance and care. When we enter a wilderness, we can experience more of who God is. We can look for him to be powerful and present and experience him in ways we can only uniquely find in those wilderness moments.

When you find yourself in a wilderness season, look around for who God is and what he is doing in the middle of it. He promises he is there.

Father God, show me where you have been in my past wilderness seasons. Come close to me now, in the season I am in, and help me to trust in your promises and your love for me. Amen

RACHEL TURNER

A land flowing with milk and honey

'So I have come down to rescue them from the hand of the Egyptians
and to bring them up out of that land into a good and spacious land,
a land flowing with milk and honey.' (NIV)

Many of our wilderness seasons can feel endless. Whether it is grief, financial struggles, illness, persecution or loneliness, we can lose hope of ever
coming out the other side.

God knew the Israelites needed hope in front of them if they were to
persevere through the desert. He didn't simply tell them that he would
rescue them and then lead them blindly into the wilderness. He laid out
for them the hope that would be at the end of the wilderness: a new home
where they could flourish and grow.

Throughout the first few books of the Bible, we watch the Israelites
as they lose belief in that hope. Their immediate circumstances looked
too big; the wilderness seemed too hard. The hope of a new home wasn't
strong enough for them to be faithful in the wilderness season, and so they
struggled with God and kicked against him. It took 40 years for them to
learn the blessings of the desert season and be ready to enter the promised land.

It can be so easy to take our eyes off our hope when we are in our wilderness seasons – hope that God will be who he says he is and that he has
a future for us that is good; hope that he has a purpose for us and loves
us; hope that the Bible is true and that God is at work. We focus on our
immediate struggles and our hope flickers, leaving us with only the desert
to look at.

Where is your hope? In a season of wilderness, what do you cling to?
How can you remind yourself of who God is and what his promises are?

---

*Father God, bring to our minds a scripture or truth that we can cling to in
our wilderness seasons. Remind us of who you are and the hope you have
set before us. Amen*

RACHEL TURNER

I am doing

'See, I am doing a new thing! Now it springs up; do you not perceive it?'
(NIV)

I am overly judgemental of people in the Bible sometimes. I read of their
fears and their doubts of God and I can quickly jump to judgement. 'Why
are they doubting God now? He *just* performed an enormous number of
miracles, and they are still afraid? I don't get it.'

I can easily forget that the people we read about are in the middle of
their wilderness stories. In this passage, the people are seemingly abandoned in a foreign land after seeing their homes destroyed and captured
by the conquering army. Elsewhere in the Bible we read about people in
a barren place with no ability to feed themselves, women wrestling with
infertility who fear they will never have the gift of a child or prophets so
discouraged and frightened that they simply want to give up. They are in
the middle of their wilderness and do not know what will happen next.

But God is at work in each of their wildernesses. In some wildernesses,
he transforms people into who he wants them to be. They are in the process of becoming. Some people's wilderness is a call to 'othering' – a place
of community and purpose where they might minister to others. Sometimes God calls people into rest and connection with him. Their wilderness
is a time to talk honestly, heal and re-establish a way of walking with God.
For others, the wilderness is a time of shaping and equipping, when God
invites them to partner with him to shape the world around them, even
when it is hard.

In every wilderness, God is at work. A wilderness is never *only* a wilderness. Let that thought encourage you as you consider where God might be
leading you today.

---

*Father God, show me how you have worked in the wildernesses of my past
and help me to see where you are at work in my life today. Amen*

RACHEL TURNER

Becoming

'Now if you obey me fully and keep my covenant, then out of all nations you will be my treasured possession. Although the whole earth is mine, you will be for me a kingdom of priests and a holy nation.'
(NIV)

Every year, I vigilantly, and slightly obsessively, look for the early signs of spring – for the first sight of the crocus poking through the hard ground on the pathway outside my home, for the tiny buds forming on the dead-looking branches on the trees outside my window. Every day, growth seems to occur.

Similarly, some wilderness experiences can be seasons of growth and transformation. Scripture provides many examples. When Jesus went into the wilderness, he was tempted by Satan. It was a crucial time for him to become ready to begin his ministry. Before he was king, David had to hide in the wilderness, scrabbling for food and terrified for his life. Over many years, God slowly transformed him from a small shepherd boy into a skilled warrior and leader. The 40 years the Israelites spent in the desert taught them how to walk with God, how to obey with courage and rely on God's leading and not their own.

For some of us, our wilderness will be a season of growth, as God takes us on a journey of becoming. Amid the struggle, God may be refining our character or giving us skills we will need for the future. He may be rooting out lies we have believed and filling us with his truth or encouraging us to do and be who he created us to be.

Are we ready to allow the mess that sometimes happens when God works to transform us and make us more like Jesus, more like who we are created to be?

Father God, we open our hearts and minds to you. Shape, prune, search and teach us, so that we may say 'yes' to the transformation you are bringing in our lives to enable us to be more like you. Amen

RACHEL TURNER

Don't look back

'Forget the former things; do not dwell on the past.' (NIV)

Twenty years ago, I faced one of the toughest wildernesses of my life. On my honeymoon, I became ill with a chronic and life-altering disease. My healthy body was ravaged, and I was confined to a wheelchair. All my dreams of my future were destroyed. It was an unexpected journey of becoming, but all I could think about was what I had lost: my health, my strength, my words, my clarity of thought, my friendships and my future. I couldn't embrace what God was doing, because all I could see was what he wasn't doing.

When God led the Israelites into the wilderness, they left the homes that their families had lived in for 400 years. They followed God into the wilderness but struggled to let go of the past. God was trying to teach them about his provision and love, providing food for them every day in the form of manna, but the Israelites couldn't stop comparing and complaining: 'If only we had meat to eat! We remember the fish we ate in Egypt at no cost – also the cucumbers, melons, leeks, onions and garlic. But now we have lost our appetite; we never see anything but this manna!' (Numbers 11: 4–5). Years into the wilderness, they could not become the community God called them to be because they kept longing for what they had known before. Their desire for the past stopped them from embracing God's miraculous provision, faithfulness and love.

When I began to let go of all I had lost in my wilderness season, I was able to go on one of the most precious spiritual journeys of my life. It shaped who I am today.

When we let go of the past, we free ourselves to embrace what God is doing in the present.

Father God, show me where my hands and heart are tied up in clinging to the past. Help me to put down what I need to release, so that I can embrace what you are doing in my life now. Amen

RACHEL TURNER

Othering

And because of my chains, most of the brothers and sisters have become confident in the Lord and dare all the more to proclaim the gospel without fear. (NIV)

'What is she doing?!' I was shocked as I scrolled through a video post on my phone one morning. It was from my friend on our Parenting for Faith social media page. She was in hospital with her newly born daughter, who was struggling to breathe independently. As I pushed the play button, I was astonished to hear her begin to talk about her experiences of God in her hospital room.

She shared her struggles and talked about finding God in the midst of it all. She encouraged other parents who may find themselves in desperate situations with their children and pointed them to God and his care.

Sometimes, in a wilderness moment, we are called to invest in others. In our reading today we meet another person in a wilderness moment. Paul was imprisoned and held back from sharing the gospel in the way he had done for so many years. And so he flung himself into 'othering'. Paul used his time in the wilderness to encourage, teach, support and connect with others. He enabled his struggles to be a testament to the truth of who God was.

Similarly, in the book of Ruth, we see two women in the depths of an intense wilderness of loss and grief who decide to love and sacrifice for each other, and eventually become part of Jesus' family line.

We may be in an 'othering' season in our own wilderness. Perhaps you are struggling with mental health, physical pain, isolation or fear, but you are still significant in others' lives, able to encourage, love and point people to God, who is at work in all circumstances.

Father God, show me who I can love, pray for or encourage in this wilderness season. Who in my life do you want me to invest in? Use me, God, for your purposes in others' lives. Amen

RACHEL TURNER

Resting

He came to a broom bush, sat down under it and prayed that he might die. 'I have had enough, Lord,' he said. 'Take my life; I am no better than my ancestors.' (NIV)

We may be mentally exhausted, spirirtually tired, emotionally drained or physically sore. Whatever the need, we can find ourselves in the wilderness, desperate for rest.

In this passage, Elijah runs into the wilderness so emotionally discouraged and frightened that he wants God to end it all. Instead, God encourages him to sleep and provides some food. They don't talk. God doesn't force Elijah to worship or study his word. Instead, God sends him the gift of sleep and snacks.

When I had my hysterectomy, the recovery was long and arduous. I was exhausted and yet ashamed that I needed rest. I swung wildly between longing for rest and forcing myself into activity to work my way into feeling better. Every day, God would whisper to me through scripture, friends and prayer about his gift of rest.

It can feel selfish to grasp a season of rest in the wilderness, but there is purpose in rest. There is healing in sleep. There is a blessing in the stillness that allows God to care for us as we allow ourselves to rest with him. In rest, we can experience what it is like to be God's child, loved and accepted just as we are. In rest, we can learn to be with God without having to do anything for him or show how much we love him with our actions. In rest, we can embrace the simple companionship and grace of a present, loving God.

In a wilderness where rest seems to be the purpose, embrace it. Your job is to rest in obedience and enjoy the ministering of God's peace in the stillness.

Father God, teach me how to rest in the wilderness. Give me your gift of sleep and provision for the rest that will restore my mind, soul, heart and body. Be with me as I sleep and rest and be. Amen

RACHEL TURNER

Water in the desert

'I provide water in the wilderness and streams in the wasteland, to give drink to my people, my chosen, the people I formed for myself that they may proclaim my praise.' (NIV)

When I was a child, my parents took me hiking in the Grand Canyon. It was over nine hours of steep trails, in 45°C heat. A hot, dry wind blew dirt and sand into our eyes as the blazing sunshine burnt our skin. I have never experienced thirst as I did on that trip. I was so afraid we would run out of water and die right there in the canyon!

Throughout the Israelites journey in the wilderness, the issue of access to water arises. In the Desert of Shur, they eventually find water, but it is unfit to drink (Exodus 15:22–25). I can't imagine the fear they would have felt in the heat and the dirt, feeling exposed and helpless. They had escaped slavery and emerged into a wilderness with no idea how to provide for themselves. They were thirsty, and there was no drinkable water in sight. I would be beside myself with fear and panic. The Israelites needed God's provision for their most basic needs in order for them to survive in the wilderness, and he was faithful to provide it every time – after 'Moses cried out to the Lord… the water became fit to drink' (Exodus 2:25).

The Bible is full of stories of God providing water for those who need it. To Abraham, Isaac, Jacob, Moses, David, Gideon, on and on, he brought water in the wilderness.

In our seasons of wilderness, we will have basic needs. Sometimes it is the need for friendship or food or perhaps a ride to hospital. God cares about these needs and many people can testify to his faithfulness and willingness to meet them. In your wilderness, may you know the God who provides water in the desert.

Father God, we lay before you our needs, both basic and complex. Give us water in the desert place and minister to our bodies, souls, minds and hearts. We trust you to provide for us. Amen

RACHEL TURNER

Connecting

Moses led the people out from the camp to meet with God, and they stood at the foot of the mountain. (NIV)

God brought the Israelites out of Egypt and into the wilderness to establish a relationship. He promised their forefathers Abraham, Isaac and Jacob that he would be their God and they would be his people. The wilderness was a reconnection between them, a time for them to find a way to be together.

Unfortunately, sin still stood between them. The people gathered around the mountain, and God came close, yet the distance between them still seemed vast. God gave his commandments to show them how to live holy lives, but they would not be able to do it. It would take another 1,500 years for Jesus to come and provide a way for sin to no longer be a barrier between God and his people.

And yet God still drew his people close to him in the desert. He created a place for his presence to live right in the middle of their camp, and he regularly talked with Moses. He ensured that his people could see him every moment by being present in a pillar of cloud by day and a pillar of fire at night. He taught them how to seek him out and how to live every day with him even while in the wilderness.

In the seasons of life that feel like a wilderness, there remains the opportunity to connect with God, draw close to him, learn how to see him and love him, and have him at the centre of our homes and lives.

A wilderness season is an opportunity to pull God close and to learn how to cling to the God who is seeking to be with you.

Father God, come close to me today. Teach me how to see you and know you in my ordinary, everyday life. Help me to keep you at the centre of my heart, that I may live close to your love and guidance. Amen

RACHEL TURNER

Lamenting

All night long I flood my bed with weeping and drench my couch with tears. (NIV)

'I'm not sure you can say that,' uttered the shy eight-year-old boy as he shifted in his seat looking around for support. The other children in the Sunday morning group nodded solemnly. We had been discussing prayer and how honest David was in his psalms to God.

The psalm we read felt so genuine, honest and unguarded that the children were unsure if it was okay to pray that way. What does it say about the way we approach and model prayer if our children think they cannot pour their emotions out to God? How many of us feel the same and hold our harsher, more raw emotions back when we pray?

I love the psalms because they express what David and others really felt. There is no pretence. David was often writing his psalms while suffering or hiding in both a physical and emotional wilderness. Whether his pain was self-inflicted or the unjust persecution of his king, David poured out his emotions and requests to God. The result is raw and beautiful.

In our wilderness times, we can drop all the pretence we often have in our prayer lives. We can be ruthlessly honest with God about our feelings, hopes, dreams, frustrations and thoughts. God longs to share our lives with us, to help us and to heal the most vulnerable parts of our hearts and minds. When we feel free to share the unvarnished truth with him, we can connect with him in the deep, dark places within ourselves.

Let us boldly lament in the wilderness seasons and experience the joy of being heard by God and understood.

Take a few moments to be honest with God about how you feel about your current situation (or someone else you are concerned about). What do you want God to do?

RACHEL TURNER

Shaping

'See, I have chosen Bezalel son of Uri, the son of Hur, of the tribe of Judah, and I have filled him with the Spirit of God, with wisdom, with understanding, with knowledge and with all kinds of skills.' (NIV)

As the Israelites learn how to walk with God in the wilderness, God announces his big plan to move into the centre of the Israelite camp so that his very presence can be among them. God is very particular about what he wants, down to the exact materials and colour of the fabric (Exodus 35:35). In the middle of this wilderness experience, God invites some individuals to work with him to shape something new. It seems that sometimes in the wilderness, God calls us by name to partner with him to achieve something on his heart.

God created us for purpose. His first statement to human beings after creating them was to explain what they were created to do (Genesis 1:28). He knows that some of us, even in a wilderness season, are eager and ready to work for him in whatever way we can. There are specific works that God is doing in our families and communities, and he may open opportunities for us that are unique to this season.

For some of us, the wilderness may be one of the most productive seasons we have. It may be parenting our children through a tough wilderness of our family life, leading a team through struggles, ministering to a lonely neighbour or stepping into a role at church.

If you see needs open up in front of you or feel inexplicably drawn to help in places, even when you are in a wilderness season, God may be calling you to partner with what he is doing. May God keep our hands and hearts free to say 'yes' to his invitations.

Father God, we want to say 'yes' to your invitation to partner with you, even during our wilderness seasons. We will follow you, God. Lead on. Amen

RACHEL TURNER

The danger of the promised land

'Now then, you and all these people, get ready to cross the River Jordan into the land I am about to give to them – to the Israelites. I will give you every place where you set your foot, as I promised Moses.' (NIV)

When we are in the wilderness of life, we can often see things more clearly. We have a greater grasp of what is important, a deeper appreciation of simple pleasures, an increased sensitivity to the sharp sting of any unsorted regrets and an intense and grateful reliance on the God who sustains us.

In the Bible, we read about how the Israelites experienced this. God performed miracles every day in feeding, shading, leading and sustaining his people through the wilderness. And he promised them that it wouldn't be forever – one day, God would lead them to the promised land. And he did. But they couldn't handle it. The new land offered much: ready-made cities, agriculture and water, riches and political power. It had everything they needed, so they learned to rely on it rather than God. The comfort of the promised land numbed them.

As I emerge from wilderness seasons, I notice this with me – normal returns. I no longer wake up distinctly aware of the sheer gift of the breath in my lungs. I no longer have to rely on God for strength and peace to sustain me through physical pain or exhaustion. I emerge into the promised land – the beautiful oasis after the wilderness.

And it scares me. I don't want the blessing of the promised land to rob me of the lessons of the wilderness.

The wilderness was brutal. And delightful. And painful. And grace-filled. I learned so much about God and myself. I was blessed and taught and shaped in the wilderness.

I have always wondered how God intended his people to live in the promised land. What would it have looked like if they had managed to live in it and still rely on him?

As seasons begin to shift, the wilderness may appear to be ending. What lessons of the wilderness do you need to wrap your arms around and hold on to?

RACHEL TURNER

Finding your feet

The day after the Passover, that very day, they ate some of the produce of the land: unleavened bread and roasted grain. The manna stopped the day after they ate this food from the land; there was no longer any manna for the Israelites. (NIV)

After 40 years in the wilderness, the Israelites finally began to step into the promised land. It had taken decades for them to become a nation of people who knew God and how to walk with him. An entire generation had passed on, and a new generation, raised in the wilderness, were now grown and ready to take on God's promises. Throughout those 40 years, their clothes and shoes never wore out, they lived within sight of God's continual presence and they woke every morning to the food they would need for the day.

And then, in a very short amount of time, that all changed. The cloud of God was no longer visible, they began to need to source their own clothing and shoes, and their food from God stopped appearing.

I sometimes try to imagine how they felt that morning when they realised they would never again taste manna. Were they so excited about the new food that the loss of the old didn't matter?

Leaving a wilderness season can be an exciting, joyful time of relief and delight. But it will be a change. God's new provision will be just as fundamental, but it may look and feel different. The new season may require more work or change how you interact with God. Coming out of the wilderness is not simply life getting better; it is one spiritual season ending and a new one beginning. It helps to take a moment to acknowledge this change and pay attention to the slight shifts that will begin to occur between you and God.

Father God, when you are ready to call me out of the wilderness, help me to put down the provisions I have known and pick up your new provisions. Guide me, God, that I might walk well with you in a new season. Amen

RACHEL TURNER

A new way

When the trumpets sounded, the army shouted, and at the sound of the trumpet, when the men gave a loud shout, the wall collapsed; so everyone charged straight in, and they took the city. (NIV)

When the Israelites came to Jericho, they were experienced fighters. Over time in the wilderness, they trained and became ready to conquer. They defeated over 60 walled cities in the neighbouring areas as they approached the promised land. Many of the cities were much more prominent than Jericho. Jericho was a small town, easily conquered by the Israelite army. But God surprised them.

He interrupted their plan and introduced his own. A plan that, on the face of it, didn't make sense. Rather than conquering the city in the way they knew how, they were to restrain themselves and do it God's way. They had to choose whether to go forward in their own knowledge and strength or follow in obedience to God. The wilderness lessons taught them to put aside their ways and follow God's.

They had been transformed by their time in the desert, from a complaining, untrusting crowd to a disciplined, unified community who fully committed to God's unusual instruction, even when it didn't make sense.

As we emerge from our wilderness seasons, many of us are eager to get back to normal. We may look at familiar tasks and situations and think, 'I know how to do this. I'll slot right back in.' But I think there is an opportunity to keep in mind here. Maybe God has new ways of doing old, familiar things. Before we pick up right where we left off, pause for a moment to listen for God's prompting on how the old things you knew how to do may be different this time around.

We need his guidance as much in the promised land as we did in the wilderness. In the wilderness, we relied on it for survival, but in the promised land, following God's guidance is an outworking of our relationship with him.

May God teach us how to embrace the wilderness seasons and walk with him in them, whether we are becoming, othering, resting, connecting, lamenting or shaping. May we cling to God and trust him, even in the wilderness.

RACHEL TURNER

Tending the mind

Sandra Wheatley writes:

When David declared, 'I am fearfully and wonderfully made' (Psalm 139: 14, NIV), he nailed it! The intricate workings of our bodies – how our hearts, kidneys and other organs function together in perfect harmony – has intrigued and fascinated me throughout my nursing career and beyond. But it is the mind that still seems to be the most mysterious and elusive. It is amazing that something both as sublime and insubstantial as thoughts or consciousness can emerge from three pounds of gelatinous pudding inside our skulls!

For centuries philosophers and scientists have debated and tussled over how to define the human mind and the human brain, and the difference between them. Is there a difference? One definition – 'the mind is the software, and the brain is the hardware'– can be a helpful illustration.

But it wasn't until the end of the 20th century that the means to see and explore just what is happening within our brains when we think, react, speak or sing could be observed. Brain-imaging technology came to the fore. It is now possible to see the living human brain at work and the impact our thinking, our emotions and our actions have on our brains. We now know that our minds are intricate and precious and are so often damaged as we encounter life and all it brings.

There isn't a day that passes without awareness being raised regarding those suffering from mental health issues. The charity Mind lists more than 32 different conditions, including anxiety, depression, anorexia, bulimia, loneliness, post-natal depression and post-traumatic stress disorder. Low self-esteem and self-harm are also part of the growing list of issues we face when our minds seem no longer able to cope with the pressures imposed upon them. Can we actively tend to and care for our minds just as we do other parts of our bodies?

Jesus said, 'Love the Lord your God with all your heart and with all your soul and with all your mind' (Matthew 22:37, NIV). Our minds are important to God and in the coming days it is my hope and prayer that we will realise just how precious our wholeness in mind, body and spirit are to him. May we learn to carefully tend to them through his word and by his Spirit.

A new pathway

Do not conform to the pattern of this world, but be transformed by the renewing of your mind. (NIV)

It seems as if we are constantly being encouraged to transform our homes, bodies and lifestyles – often at immense financial cost. It is easy to feel pressured to change and conform to a pattern set by society and social media.

The transformation and renewal Paul is speaking of is something more radical, ongoing and lifelong. The Greek word for transformation is *metamorphoses*. The glorious process of a stunning butterfly emerging from a caterpillar chrysalis is a lovely illustration of such a transformation.

Can something as beautiful and transformative be possible for us and can it really start within our minds?

Our thought patterns do have a significant effect upon our brains and our behaviour. The power of our mind to change the brain is called neuroplasticity – spiritually we call it 'renewing the mind'!

Is this possible? A simple analogy of what can be a difficult and challenging process is to picture a pathway through the woods. The more we walk along it the clearer and wider it becomes and easier to access. But if we stopped walking along the path, it would become overgrown and be more difficult to find.

It is the same with our neural pathways. The more we think about something repeatedly, the more our neural connections become stronger and thoughts are easier to access. This is not what we want when those thoughts are toxic and negative. We need to stop that particular pattern of thinking and then that pathway will become overgrown and inaccessible.

With the help of the Holy Spirit, our 'paraclete', our 'alongsider', we can replace negative thoughts with thoughts of the love and the goodness of God from his word. Gradually we will find ourselves walking a path that does transform and renew, not only our minds but also our lives!

Father God, so many times my thoughts seem to be like a dense undergrowth. By your Holy Spirit please help me to clear that path and renew my thinking. Amen

SANDRA WHEATLEY

Taking hold

Do not be anxious about anything, but in every situation, by prayer and petition, with thanksgiving, present your requests to God. (NIV)

The word 'anxious' is from the Greek word *merimnao*, meaning 'to take thought'. It's the same word Jesus uses in Matthew 6:25: 'Take no thought for… what ye shall eat, or… put on' (KJV).

We are bombarded with thoughts every waking moment. Even now our brains are processing a myriad of signals and thoughts, memories of the past, wonderings about the future or just random thoughts of loved ones and the day ahead.

When thoughts rush in it's difficult not to 'take' the ones that cause distress and anxiety. It's hard to swat them away before they 'take root'.

Yesterday, we saw that our minds have the ability to create new pathways. Can we tend those pathways as we would a garden? Gardening is hard work! It takes time and energy to prepare the soil and remove rocks and weeds to ensure everything is ready for new plants and seeds. It takes lots of patience and care until we see transformation and new growth.

More so with our fragile minds. They can be a minefield at times. The thing about a minefield is that you don't know where the mines are… until you detonate one.

When we're in the midst of that daily, hourly battle against those incendiary thoughts of doubt, failure or rejection with which the enemy of our soul plagues us, is it possible to 'take no thought'?

I believe it is – but it isn't easy. Our first key is repetition – especially the repetition of scriptures! We can ask the Holy Spirit to remind us of scriptures that bring hope, light in our darkness and the truth of who we really are in Christ. Then 'take hold' of those scriptures and repeat them again and again.

Our hard work will pay off, transformation will come through the work of the Holy Spirit and God's word.

Father God, our tender gardener, help us to allow your word to be planted into our minds once again today. Amen

SANDRA WHEATLEY

It's a battle

We demolish arguments… and we take captive every thought to make it obedient to Christ. (NIV)

Paul introduces another strategy to us in the 'how-to' of tending and protecting our minds from the daily onslaughts they face.

It really is fighting talk. Paul knew what a battleground our minds can be and how 'strongholds' in our mindset can seem almost impregnable.

Some of us may struggle with a poor self-image, which leads us to see ourselves as being less able, less attractive, always messing up or too sinful to be loved by God. These thoughts can become strongholds of doubt, fear and inadequacy. They grip our fragile minds and convince us we'll never be free.

It starts with a thought: a simple innocuous thought that becomes a pretension – an 'assertion of a claim to something' (*Oxford English Dictionary*) – then becomes an argument and then a stronghold – a habitual pattern of thought.

In the garden of Eden, a seed of doubt was planted in Eve's mind by Satan, 'Did God really say…?' he asked in Genesis 3:1. And he is still doing the same today. 'Did God really say you are loved, forgiven, safe, cherished, called by him?'

A thought planted, a pathway opened and a stronghold created. But, as verse 4 reminds us, the 'weapons' we have from God have divine power to demolish these strongholds. When we recognise them, see them for what they are and allow that recognition to be the light that exposes them, they become more and more ineffectual. Again, as we ask the Holy Spirit to bring to mind scriptures that counter the lies of the enemy and expose those negative things we feel about ourselves, then gradually this battle will be won. We will know this assurance and truth: 'And the peace of God, which transcends all understanding, will guard your hearts and your minds in Christ Jesus' (Philippians 4:7).

Father God, please guard my heart and mind today as I trust in you. Amen
SANDRA WHEATLEY

Fill your mind with goodness

Finally, brothers and sisters, whatever is true, whatever is noble, whatever is right… whatever is lovely… think about such things. (NIV)

Paul tells us that we will be 'transformed by the renewing of your mind' (Romans 12:2), and I find it fascinating that neuroscience confirms that he was on to something big! Remember neuroplasticity from Sunday's note – the brain's ability to change based on how we think and behave? We now know that our brains do structurally change as a result of the input they receive. It's amazing that research on the brain is verifying what Paul spoke of centuries ago!

Yesterday we saw that doing battle with the thoughts and lies the enemy bombards us with isn't easy. Yet Paul helps us again in directing us to think about those things that are true, noble, right, pure and lovely in order to override those thoughts of despair, helplessness and fear.

I heard a story of a man who struggled desperately with a drinking habit. Every evening he'd return home inebriated, despairing of being able to change. One day he noticed a café next door to the pub and decided to go inside. He ordered a glass of milk, then another and another until he felt too full to drink anything else! As he emerged hours later, he defiantly shook his fist at the devil saying, 'I'm too full of milk now to be able to drink anything else!'

Can we do the same by filling our minds with the 'milk' of scripture?

Years ago, dear friends encouraged me to do this. They reminded me of Romans 8:28, encouraging me to know that God was in control of my life and working out his purposes. And then, as my situation worsened, Romans 8:35–39 became my lifeline – nothing can or ever will separate me from God!

These are some of my go-to verses, precious seeds planted long ago, still bearing fruit.

Father God, thank you for those who have helped me to tend my fragile mind with your word and truth. Help me to help others in doing likewise. Amen

SANDRA WHEATLEY

Don't forget to remember

Yet this I call to mind and therefore I have hope: Because of the Lord's great love we are not consumed, for his compassions never fail. (NIV)

Memory is a central theme in scripture in both the Old and New Testaments. The Israelites were instructed to remember their deliverance from slavery and to pass on those memories to future generations.

At the last supper, Jesus invited his disciples to enter into a new covenant and to 'do this in remembrance of me' (Luke 22:19).

Clearly it is important that we engage in times of remembering, to reminisce with others – and with God. Memory is precious, but it is also fragile.

We have no filing cabinet of memories in our brains. Instead, various parts of our brains have different roles to play in what is remembered – and what is forgotten.

Sadly, just like any other organ, our brains are susceptible to disease and injury, with perhaps one of the most familiar and distressing being Alzheimer's disease. Over 850,000 people and families in the UK are affected by this horrible and cruel disease. Many reading these notes will be aware of its devastating impact on their lives.

Can we tend to the minds of those we love dearly who are being snatched away from us as their memories, thoughts and behaviour change radically?

There are no easy answers. But I can testify that I saw precious moments of awareness ignited as I sat alongside my mum and other friends affected by dementia and started to sing old, familiar hymns. Their agitation and distress subsided as they joined in singing hymns that were seemingly forgotten – and recalled and recited scriptures too. These were lives 'kept by the power of God' (1 Peter 1:5, KJV).

I believe God continues to make himself known to our loved ones affected by dementia or Alzheimer's.

Dear Lord, we entrust to you again our loved ones affected by the cruellest of diseases. Thank you that they continue to be known and loved by you. Amen
SANDRA WHEATLEY

Tending our minds through prayer

Rejoice always, pray continually, give thanks in all circumstances; for this is God's will for you in Christ Jesus. (NIV)

In writing this short series I've realised again just how much I don't know! And how much I delight in discovering new things and gaining a new understanding of God, the scriptures and us. I have also learned how much current research and discoveries validate scripture.

A relatively new field of learning and research is neurotheology – the study of the relationship between the brain and religious practices. MRI studies of the brain have shown that when we pray, the frontal cortex of our brain lights up, and the more we pray the more neural pathways are created and strengthened. Paul really was on to something when he encouraged us to 'pray continually'.

I love this quote from Martin Luther: 'I have so much to do that I must spend the first three hours of each day in prayer!' (Though for me it is more an aspiration than a daily reality.)

The Bible speaks so much about prayer and its power in our lives, but how, in these busy, frenetic lives of ours, do we tend to our minds through prayer? One of the most powerful ways to pray is to incorporate verses of scripture in our prayers and pray them back to God. When we pray in this way, we are encouraged both through hearing the word of God and knowing we are using the most powerful weapon there is – God's living word – against the enemy of our souls.

It only takes a few moments and can be something we repeat throughout the day as our prayer and memory verse. In this way, just a few seconds of your personal devotional time can have a powerful effect on your mind, body and spirit.

Father God, I know you will keep me in your perfect peace as I keep my mind focused on you (Isaiah 26:3). Amen

SANDRA WHEATLEY

And finally...

Finally, believers, whatever is true... think *continually* on these things (centre your mind on them, and implant them in your heart). (AMP)

Just about every news bulletin on TV or the radio finishes with, 'And finally...' and then a story is told that often becomes *the* item that stays in our mind. So I hope it is okay to revisit this verse in closing our week together and that this 'finally' will stay with you – and bless you.

Who or what do you think of as you read this verse? For me, the 'whatever' becomes a 'whoever', and that 'whoever' is the only person I know who is true, noble, right, pure and lovely. He is admirable, excellent and praiseworthy. He is Jesus. My Jesus, my Saviour.

Colossians 3:2 encourages us to 'set your minds on things above' (NIV), which isn't easy. Our minds are assailed by thoughts and images of a world that is seemingly edging further away from God, and we face challenges that seem overwhelming. But if we can begin that process of renewing our minds, believing that memorising scripture and praying does physiologically make a difference to our brains, just as Paul said it would, then transformation will certainly come.

I came across this anonymous quote recently: 'What the mind attends to, it considers. What the mind does not attend it to, it dismisses. What the mind attends to continually, it believes. What the mind believes, it eventually does.'

It is a stark choice: to believe that all God has said about us is true and all Jesus did for us is complete, or to take those seeds of doubt and lies the devil tries to plant in our minds and allow them to take root. What our minds believe we will eventually do, by the power of the Holy Spirit and the truths of God's word.

Ours is the most incredible of journeys as we walk with God. Transformation will come. Be patient with yourself – God is.

Father God, may we know your presence and enabling grace as we believe you will help us to renew and tend to our mind's day by day. Change will come. In Jesus' name. Thank you, Lord. Amen

SANDRA WHEATLEY

The wives of the patriarchs

Elaine Storkey writes:

The first five books of the Hebrew scriptures introduce us to the record of the people of Israel beginning from the earliest times and stretching down through the generational lines. We read lengthy genealogies and cover hundreds of years of history. Yet the text offers us far more than abstract lists of complicated and difficult names! People come to life in front of us as we're introduced to the families they lived in and the challenges they faced. Through their stories, we get a real insight into the kind of people they were and how they understood the call of God in their lives.

Israel was a patriarchal society. That means that its leadership and authority was vested in the male heads of the tribal families. Authority was passed down from patriarch to patriarch as the mantle of leadership fell on the firstborn son of the next generation. The stories of Abraham, Isaac and Jacob, and their response to God, was to anchor the history of the Israelites for future centuries. Yet, though the structure was patriarchal, women were by no means ignored in the biblical text. The authors of the Pentateuch paid special attention to the wives of the patriarchs as well as introducing us to the lives of many other women. The actions of Sarah, Hagar, Rebecca, Leah and Rachel, their response to God and their lives as mothers, would themselves be significant in shaping the history of a nation.

The narratives of the different wives of the patriarchs often overlap, with occurrences curiously repeated in subsequent generations. Lessons, it seems, are not always learnt. What is more, the text discloses to us several incidents in their stories which are to the detriment of their husbands; both weakness and cowardice mar the men's obedience in following God. Yet we should not be surprised to find these episodes recorded, for the Bible shows no interest in preserving the reputation of the male leaders when their faults were glaringly obvious. The women too were not always paragons of virtue; alongside their many good qualities, we read of jealousy, favouritism, cruelty and deceit. So, in these Bible stories we find people who embody both the potential and the failings of the human race. What is remarkable is that, despite their failings, God blesses them and uses them to fulfil his promises. We should be encouraged that God can do the same with us.

Sarai faces an uncertain future

Terah took his son Abram, his grandson Lot son of Haran, and his daughter-in-law Sarai, the wife of his son Abram, and together they set out from Ur of the Chaldeans to go to Canaan. (NIV)

The text says little here about Sarai's ancestry; we know from Genesis 20:12 that she was Abram's half-sister as well as his wife. She clearly belonged to the race of Semites, the Chaldeans, who had lived in Ur for hundreds of years. So we can imagine the uncertainty she felt when Terah and Abram announced they would all take the mammoth journey from Ur to Canaan. It meant leaving her ancestral home, travelling far away to somewhere unknown and unimaginable. Whatever her reaction and concern, she had little choice in the matter. The men held the authority and had made the decision.

Today Ur is a barren desert with ruins under the sands. Then it was a capital city, a thriving metropolis. Its stately palaces, imposing towers, law courts, markets and gardens must have produced both familiarity and security for Sarai. Located northwest of the Persian Gulf (now in Iran) with canal access to the Gulf and the Indian Ocean, it was also an international trading centre. Life in Ur was prosperous. So why should they leave?

Sarai probably knew the reason. Ur was also a place of idolatry, where hundreds of gods competed for worship. Terah's family worshipped the one God who had told Abram that he would lead them to another land and make them a great nation (12:1). Yet we can imagine the weight of Sarai's confusion and apprehension. Since she was childless and getting on in years, did God's plans exclude her?

Upheaval and change produce doubt and anxiety for us too. These are normal human reactions, especially when we have no choice. Apprehension about what lies ahead is so often mirrored in our own experience today. The challenge Sarai faced of trusting God can be real in all our lives.

Lord, help me today to let go of any anxiety about the future. Please lift my fears and teach me to trust you in every area of my life. Amen

ELAINE STORKEY

Sarai at risk through Abram's cowardice

'When the Egyptians see you, they will say, "This is his wife." Then they will kill me but will let you live. Say you are my sister, so that I will be treated well for your sake and my life will be spared because of you.' (NIV)

Having finally reached their destination it must have been disheartening for the family to find the land stricken by famine. Their itinerary had not included Egypt, but now they needed to go there for food. Abram clearly distrusted the Egyptians. So, as the husband of an attractive wife, fear for his personal safety led him to persuade Sarai to pose as his sister. The ruse worked. She was taken into Pharaoh's palace and Abram benefited from the sheep, cattle, donkeys, camels and servants he got in exchange!

The text doesn't tell us why Pharaoh suspected that diseases then inflicted on his family were related to Sarai, nor how he realised she was Abram's wife. Nevertheless, his prompt action made sure that no further damage was done, either to his household or Sarai. His angry rebuke and quick dismissal of Abram indicates how keen he was to forget the whole incident.

We're not told how Sarai felt about being badly treated by her husband. Nothing in the text suggests she consented to join Pharaoh's harem, and Abram's interest was not remotely in her well-being but in his safety and gain. He even learns little, for this same deceit is repeated in chapter 20. A Jewish commentator on the passage insists, 'There's no way that I, as a Jewish woman, can stand by the idea that it's okay to treat women as possessions instead of people.' Christian women agree!

We shouldn't be surprised at these stories, for the Bible is set in patriarchal times. And we know from other biblical passages in the Old Testament that this is not the way God sees women. In the New Testament, God's heart for women is demonstrated powerfully when Jesus regularly repudiates the culture and affirms the intrinsic worth of women. Women can live knowing God's love.

Help us, Lord, to be followers always of your truth and to be unafraid of expressing it even in challenging situations. Amen

ELAINE STORKEY

Sarai and Hagar: conflict and abuse

So after Abram had been living in Canaan ten years, Sarai his wife took her Egyptian slave Hagar and gave her to her husband to be his wife. He slept with Hagar, and she conceived. When she knew she was pregnant, she began to despise her mistress. (NIV)

Sarai's idea was to have a baby by surrogacy. After ten years in Canaan and despite repeated promises from God, she was still childless. Having a younger woman as a slave meant she could use Hagar's womb to start her family. It probably wasn't easy for Sarai to share her husband's bed with another woman. What's more, she hadn't bargained for the fact that because barrenness was a stigma, success in conceiving would give Hagar emotional capital. Even though these had been Sarai's instructions, Hagar's pregnancy compounded Sarai's humiliation. Her response was to mete out such cruelty that her slave fled.

God's compassion on Hagar mirrors his compassion on many who suffer injustice and oppression. He sends an angel to minister to her, to promise she will be the mother of descendants too numerous to count. She should return confidently and submit to Sarai. The other part of the angel's prophecy is more sober, however. Her son, Ishmael, will be a man of conflict and hostility with everyone's hand against him.

We learn other things from Hagar's story. We see why the New Testament strongly advocates monogamy as God's plan for marriage. Polygamy not only distorts the one-flesh intimacy of marriage, but also increases the potential for jealousy and strife between competing wives. We see too why so many biblical authors speak up for vulnerable people whose lives are controlled by others. Hagar represents all the women subject to sexual exploitation, who have no voice and no alternative but to comply. Her story reminds us again why sex slavery must be combatted and eradicated.

Many Christian initiatives today work with vulnerable women, trapped in different forms of sexual exploitation. They need our prayers and support. One of them is Beyond the Streets. Find out more at **beyondthestreets.org.uk**

ELAINE STORKEY

Sarah's cynicism turns to joy

Then the Lord said to Abraham, 'Why did Sarah laugh and say, "Will I really have a child, now that I am old?" Is anything too hard for the Lord? I will return to you at the appointed time next year, and Sarah will have a son.' (NIV)

Once Ishmael had been born, Abraham seemed content to see him as the child of God's promise. But God has a different plan and assures him (chapter 17) that the great nation will come through Isaac, a son promised to Sarah, who will become the father of twelve rulers. It is as a sign of this covenant that the name of Sarai ('she who strives') is changed to Sarah, meaning 'princess' (17:15). This is all in Sarah's absence, however, and when she overhears angelic visitors who have come to confirm this to Abraham, she laughs in disbelief (18:12). She's wanted a child for so many years, but at her age, the very idea is surely nonsense.

We can understand why Sarah dismisses the news. The only way this would be possible is through some miracle. And if God was not inclined to grant her a child during her fertile years, why should she believe he would now? I've been with many women for whom trying to become pregnant has been a rollercoaster and consumed so much emotional and spiritual energy. After a third miscarriage, one friend told me tearfully but resolutely, 'That's it. I'm finished. I can't go through this again.' In fact, four years later, mid-career, she did become pregnant unexpectedly. Telling almost nobody until full-term, she wonderfully gave birth to a healthy baby, and felt, in retrospect, this was the perfect timing.

God's promise to Sarah was fulfilled and Isaac was born (21:1). The story retells that Sarah laughed again; now she laughed not cynically at God's promise, but joyfully because of it. Life is not always predictable. God sometimes surprises us too, even pouring out blessings that we might have given up ever hoping for.

Write down some of the things that sometimes make you doubt God's love, and then ask God to give you a deeper understanding of his purposes.

ELAINE STORKEY

Hagar and God's covenant

Sarah saw that the son whom Hagar the Egyptian had borne to Abraham was mocking, and she said to Abraham, 'Get rid of that slave woman and her son, for that woman's son will never share in the inheritance with my son Isaac.' (NIV)

We might have thought that Sarah's antipathy towards Hagar would have changed once her own son was born. But, given that Ishmael was Abraham's older son, her insecurity remained, so she wanted the problem out of the way. With Abraham's reluctant compliance, once again Hagar became a fugitive in the desert. This time she was evicted from the household and her anxiety was for her boy, not for herself. With no other resources once the precious water ration was used up, the inevitability of his death overwhelmed her.

Abraham had fallen in with Sarah's wishes, not willingly, but because of God's permission (v. 12). So, God again stepped into the crisis facing Hagar. As before, Hagar hears God's promise to her and finds divine care and compassion. Wonderfully, as Hagar is removed from the orbit of those who controlled her, she experiences instead a deep personal relationship with God. Her identity is no longer that of an Egyptian slave, but that of a woman of significance in God's covenant with his people.

The provision of the well of water is symbolic of all the provisions God will make in the lives of Hagar and Ishmael. They will not live in opulence, but under divine protection. Ishmael will live in the Desert of Paran, Hagar will return to Egypt and find a wife for her son. And Hagar, the former concubine, will be remembered as matriarch of multiple Arab tribes and one of the key women in the Abrahamic traditions.

Hagar's story has brought encouragement to many marginalised women. A colleague of mine who leads Bible studies with women trapped in prostitution in Ethiopia's capital city found they strongly identified with her struggles. Through Hagar, many oppressed people have found for themselves that justice is close to the heart of God.

Are there areas of your life where other people are holding you back from a deeper relationship with God? Ask God to help you to know greater depth and joy in your walk with him.

ELAINE STORKEY

Rebekah wins hearts

Before he had finished praying, Rebekah came out with her jar…
She was the daughter of Bethuel son of Milkah, who was the wife of
Abraham's brother Nahor. The woman was very beautiful, a virgin…
She went down to the spring, filled her jar and came up again. (NIV)

Rebekah's entry into the family of the covenant is a wonderful story. We note Abraham and Sarah's faithfulness in wanting a bride for Isaac from their kin who worship God, rather than the idol-worshipping Canaanites they live among. We're challenged by the commitment and prayerfulness of the servant entrusted with the task of taking the long journey back to Nahor and finding this bride. We witness the hospitality of Bethuel and Laban, and their discernment in seeing God in this plan. And we're inspired by Rebekah's readiness to go in faith with the servant. God speaks into the hearts and minds of his covenant people and leads them into a new generation of service.

The story's details are significant. The servant asks God for a very specific event to eliminate any doubt of God's leading. And Rebekah, the beautiful granddaughter of Nahor, fulfils it beautifully. Her kindness to the stranger, her willingness to water his camels and commend her family's hospitality demonstrate qualities longed for by Isaac's family. The counter-cultural way Bethuel and Laban leave the final decision to Rebekah echoes God's freedom for women. And Rebekah's willingness to trust God is a challenge to all believers. The picture of Isaac meditating before he sees the servant returning with his new bride rounds off this story of faithful response to God's call. Their marriage, which appears to have been mono-gamous, became the means of the fulfilment of God's covenant to Israel.

Here Rebekah embodies the self-giving attitudes which God asks all believers to emulate. The love, joy, peace, patience, kindness, goodness, faithfulness, gentleness and self-control, which the apostle Paul describes as the fruit of the Holy Spirit, are portrayed in her already. May we know these ourselves and bear abundant fruit in our lives.

Lord, help me today to see where I need more compassion for other people, and help me to allow your Spirit to work in my own heart so I can show this more effectively in my life. Amen

ELAINE STORKEY

Rebekah's symbolic pregnancy

Isaac prayed to the Lord on behalf of his wife, because she was childless. The Lord answered his prayer, and his wife Rebekah became pregnant. The babies jostled each other within her, and she said, 'Why is this happening to me?' So she went to enquire of the Lord. (NIV)

Sarah's story of early infertility seems duplicated in Rebekah's story. But the similarity soon ends. Rebekah does not abuse another woman to use her womb, and Isaac does not take another wife. Instead, prayer provides the answer and Rebekah conceives. Her pregnancy, however, seems fraught with internal discomfort. And when God discloses the deeper meaning of what is going on inside her, it must have been a difficult explanation to grasp.

The struggle in Rebekah's womb is symbolic of the struggle that will ensue throughout the lives of the twins she is carrying, not simply around personal relationships, but also on a larger political scale. The twins will produce two nations in conflict, and the older will serve the younger. When the babies are born, yet more symbolic evidence affirms that. The second-born, Jacob, is pulling his brother Esau back, his hand firmly on his heel.

As the sons grow, their parents seemingly develop different relationships with them. Rebekah favours Jacob, but Isaac's preference is, like tradition, towards his firstborn. He identifies with Esau's prowess and hunting skills, and apparently overlooks his erratic nature and disregard for future responsibilities. He may not have known that Esau sold his first-born privileges to his brother simply for instant food. Rebekah, however, would always remember God's prediction and realise that the future outworking of God's covenant lay with Jacob's reliability and constancy.

This story challenges the view that God always calls the husband to lead the wife and be the key decision maker. Although Isaac holds authority over his wife in the patriarchy, God has revealed their future to Rebekah rather than to him. God does not reinforce human cultures but has divine plans and calls us to listen. It is a lesson we often need to remember ourselves.

Lord, help us to discern your leading on our lives and our cultures. Please give us the courage and prayerfulness to stay faithful to you in whatever situation we find ourselves in today. Amen

ELAINE STORKEY

89

Rebekah: obedience through deception?

Rebekah took the best clothes of her elder son Esau… and put them on her younger son Jacob. She also covered his hands and the smooth part of his neck with the goatskins. Then she handed to her son Jacob the tasty food and the bread she had made. (NIV)

The marriage of Rebekah and Isaac was not without friction. Like his father, Isaac passed his wife off as his sister in a crisis, though nothing came of it (chapter 26). But when Isaac was blind from old age, Rebekah constructed an elaborate deception to ensure Jacob received the blessing and inheritance of the older brother instead of Esau.

Her motives were not simply directed by favouritism. Jacob was responsible and faithful, honouring the family covenant with God by not taking Hittite wives like Esau. He had also already bought the privileges of firstborn from his brother, and it's not clear what Esau was entitled to retain through his father's blessing. So, when Rebekah outlined details for the subterfuge, Jacob willingly cooperated. Rebekah knew that Isaac would welcome delicious, cooked meats from his son, and that Jacob, dressed in Esau's clothes with goatskin on his neck and hands, could carry off the identity of the other. She also guessed that when Isaac and Esau discovered the deceit, their anger would not be directed at her.

Her plan worked. Jacob was blessed and established as heir. Now, Rebekah's task was to prevent her sons from shedding blood. She used Jacob's need for a Hebrew wife to persuade Isaac to send him with further blessings to her brother, Laban. What she could not do, of course, was soften Esau's resentment and sense of betrayal. He would be left to resolve that in future consequences.

The incident shows that women can bring about God's will, even when it means overturning the accepted order in a patriarchal culture. Yet it also raises ethical questions about deceit and manipulation. The fact that Jacob had to flee from his aggrieved brother signifies that deception is wrong. It is not commended by God, either then or now, in the lives of believers.

What do you think prevents us from having more honest relationships where we can communicate openly with each other? If these barriers exist in any of your relationships, bring them to God and pray they might be overcome.

ELAINE STORKEY

Rachel: shepherd and cousin

Then Jacob kissed Rachel and began to weep aloud. He had told Rachel that he was a relative of her father and a son of Rebekah. So she ran and told her father. (NIV)

Seeing flocks at the end of his long journey, Jacob was delighted to find they belonged to his mother's brother. But that delight was nothing compared with his ecstasy in meeting their shepherd. From their first encounter, Rachel made a huge impression on him. His tears were clearly of thankfulness at finding relatives and joy at knowing he had already met the woman he wanted to marry. The ritual of rolling away the well stone for her and watering his uncle's sheep was a practical reflection of the fact that he belonged there. Rachel clearly was also delighted to meet this new cousin and couldn't wait to tell her father.

Over the next month Rachel had ample opportunity to assess Jacob. He worked for her father without pay and no doubt found ways of expressing his admiration for her. We don't know whether Rachel had brothers, but she must have appreciated Jacob's helpfulness on her behalf. So, when Jacob and Laban came to their financial arrangement, she may well have been pleased to find she was at the centre of it.

Seven years' work in exchange for the hand in marriage of the boss' daughter doesn't sound a good deal in our modern work climate. Yet in many parts of the world the bride price, or conversely the dowry, still reflect the way marriage and economics are tied up together. Nevertheless, even then it was a bargain indeed for Laban. He gained years of willing labour and then a prized son-in-law. Yet what did Rachel think? Seven years of celibacy would be unheard of today for a couple in love, living under the same roof. Perhaps Rachel's story could help our culture realise that sex is not compulsory!

Today we live in expectation of instant gratification, where we can order what we want with a single click. Let's pray that God will also give us patience to learn the discipline of waiting when this is God's will.

ELAINE STORKEY

91

Leah: the wrong wife

So Laban brought together all the people of the place and gave a feast. But when evening came, he took his daughter Leah and brought her to Jacob, and Jacob made love to her... When morning came, there was Leah! (NIV)

The text leaves us to guess at Leah's feelings when she was instructed by her father to sleep with the intended bridegroom on what should have been her sister's wedding night. Was she worried about the betrayal? She will have been aware for all those years that Rachel was the one promised to Jacob. Yet, having been always overshadowed by her younger sister, was there now some pleasure at being the one who slept with him first?

Although it was passed off by Laban as 'custom', this action effectively forced Jacob into polygamy. He was clearly intending to marry one woman and that woman was Rachel. But by making love to her sister, Jacob was now established as married to Leah. Leah may have been afraid when the deception was disclosed, knowing that Jacob had not chosen to marry her. Yet as he continued as her husband for the week, following protocol and offering due respect, those times together may have raised strong feelings in Leah of intimacy she had never experienced before. Then she had to relinquish Jacob to the bride he really wanted.

It is clear as the story continues that although she knew she was the less-favoured wife, Leah wanted to be married to Jacob. Marriage and motherhood gave Leah status in a patriarchal world where an unmarried woman had little. She also played a significant part in the fulfilment of God's covenantal promise to Abraham, for Leah's sons, along with Rachel's, would become central in their nation's growth. Yet the jealousy Leah had probably always felt towards her younger, more beautiful sister was reinforced and would extend to the generation beyond. We see why God's plan for marriage of 'leaving and cleaving' in faithful monogamy offers a more stable structure to all family relationships.

Jacob's priorities were to serve Laban and work for the wife he believed God had given him. What would you describe as the main priorities of your life? How does God help you to accomplish these?

ELAINE STORKEY

Leah enjoys God's compassion

When the Lord saw that Leah was not loved, he enabled her to conceive, but Rachel remained childless. Leah became pregnant and gave birth to a son. She named him Reuben, for she said, 'It is because the Lord has seen my misery. Surely my husband will love me now.' (NIV)

In the culture in which they lived, Leah's fertility was her greatest asset. It was crucial that Leah was able to conceive and that offspring, especially sons, were born to Jacob. The text interprets this as a gift from God, to compensate Leah for the fact that her husband loved his other wife and not her. She wryly named her firstborn Reuben to display her value in pro-creation: 'See, a son!' Rachel's difficulty in conceiving made Leah's success more momentous, especially when she went on to bear Jacob three further sons: Simeon, Levi and Judah. The elation of giving birth to much-wanted children is something that women have felt throughout history. Yet, sadly, for Leah motherhood was tinged with a different kind of longing. After each of the first three births she spoke of her misery at not being loved by her husband, finally expressing: 'Now at last my husband will become attached to me, because I have borne him three sons.'

Even today we understand why childbirth for Leah seemed spoilt by longing and regret. In our culture women and men marry mostly because they love each other, and where a marriage is stable and mutually loving a woman can recognise she is cherished. But in any culture, marriage without love brings sorrow. That is why it is good to hear the different note sounded with the birth of Leah's fourth son. It is as if she has finally been able to enter the joy of motherhood unabated and fully return her thanks to God. 'This time I will praise the Lord.' Loneliness does pervade 'intimate' relationships where tenderness or affection are absent. Yet, love also comes in many forms and through many relationships. The blessing of children is one of the greatest means of love in anyone's life.

Loneliness is often best overcome by reaching out to other people. Who do you know who might value a call, prayer or message from you today? Pray that God might use you to help alleviate the loneliness of others.

ELAINE STORKEY

Leah and Rachel: competitive childbearing

During wheat harvest, Reuben went into the fields and found some mandrake plants, which he brought to his mother Leah. Rachel said to Leah, 'Please give me some of your son's mandrakes.' But she said to her, 'Wasn't it enough that you took away my husband? Will you take my son's mandrakes too?' (NIV)

The jealousy between the two sisters becomes explicit in this chapter. When Jacob rebukes the distressed Rachel, feeling blamed for her child-lessness, she follows the pattern of Jacob's grandmother Sarah and sends her maid Bilhah to sleep with him, 'acquiring' two sons, Dan and Naphtali. But the competition continues. Leah responds by sending her maid, Zilpah, to Jacob, and two further sons, Gad and Asher, are then attributed to Leah.

The incident over the mandrake plants makes it clear how much Leah resents Rachel, despite being well ahead in the son score. Her reference to Rachel taking her husband away is hardly fair, since Jacob had intended to marry Rachel from the beginning. The meanness over the mandrake plants seems trivial also, except, of course, that they are a fertility drug. Nevertheless, Leah uses them as an economic bargaining tool, a way of 'hiring' more marital time with their husband. Resulting sons five and six, Issacar and Zebulun, increase her advantage over her sister. The total score of sons stands at eight attributed to Leah, and only two to Rachel, through her maid. A daughter, Dinah, completes Leah's family.

When Rachel finally becomes pregnant, her reaction is different from Leah's. No hope is expressed that now her husband will love or honour her; he does that already. Her response is, 'God has taken away my disgrace.' By giving birth to Joseph, Rachel's shame disappears. We understand this today. In many parts of our world childlessness remains a stigma for women, especially in cultures where sons are prized. Even in 'progres-sive' cultures women without children can feel diminished. Motherhood is enriching and blessed by God. But it's not the only calling for women.

Children are not always cherished. Please pray for the 81,000 children in the UK care system and for those who end up homeless when they leave care. Pray that God will raise up more Christian foster homes and adoptive parents.
ELAINE STORKEY

Rachel steals the household gods

Now Rachel had taken the household gods and put them inside her camel's saddle and was sitting on them. Laban searched through everything in the tent but found nothing. Rachel said to her father, 'Don't be angry, my lord, that I cannot stand up in your presence; I'm having my period.' (NIV)

Rachel and Leah are united for once. They're both outraged at the way their father has treated them and Jacob, feeling they've missed out on the inheritance and that Laban has not paid Jacob properly for 20 years' work. Jacob, however, has remedied this by carefully propagating speckled and spotted livestock which Laban agreed should be his. Now Jacob and his wives prepare to follow God's instruction to leave Laban and take their children, livestock and goods back to Jacob's family home. Just before they leave, Rachel steals her father's household gods, the teraphim.

We're not told why. The teraphim were not pagan idols, but related in some way to Hebrew worship and would have been family property for years, so perhaps Rachel wanted them as a keepsake. They could also have been valuable. Whichever it was, the theft inflamed the already fraught situation. Laban pursued Jacob and caught up with the family, but obeyed God in being conciliatory. Simply sharing his hurt at their abrupt departure, the theft became Laban's focus. Rachel's wrongdoing could have had dire consequences, especially when Jacob pronounced a death sentence on the thief. Her appeal to her period ensured the theft went undetected.

The reconciliation between Laban and Jacob took place despite Rachel. Her cover-up became necessary for her own security, but God effectively led the men to a peaceful conclusion, sharing food, blessing each other and making promises for the future. It was God's mercy towards the family that covered the wrongdoing and let the guilty one walk free. Rachel's guilt reminds us that for us too, God's grace, mercy and love are so much greater than we deserve.

Let's ask God to make us more intentional in living according to his will, perhaps reflecting on things that we feel we could have done better recently, or remarks made to others that might have been kinder.

ELAINE STORKEY

Rachel again in childbirth

While they were still some distance from Ephrath, Rachel began to give birth and had great difficulty. And as she was having great difficulty in childbirth, the midwife said to her, 'Don't despair, for you have another son.' As she breathed her last – for she was dying – she named her son Ben-Oni. (NIV)

Rachel had been Jacob's favoured wife throughout their marriage and had known his constant protection over her. This was evident even at the potentially traumatic meeting with defrauded brother, Esau, when Jacob placed Rachel and Joseph as far away as possible from danger (33:2–3). Now, with the brothers reunited and the symbolic return of the family to Bethel (35:3–7), Rachel became pregnant for the second time. The pregnancy itself was an answer to Rachel's longings, not merely because her sister had produced more offspring than she, but because she loved her husband deeply and wanted to give him a second son.

So, the future for the family looked full of hope. God changed Jacob's name to Israel and renewed the promises of land and nation. It must have felt to them all that the covenant with Abraham was close to being fully realised. When they paused their journey for Rachel's labour, they probably expected another safe childbirth. The midwife expressed words of encouragement, but the outcome was different. Rachel's name for her baby, 'son of my trouble,' reflected more than birth difficulties. It conveyed joy for a son, but sorrow as her life ebbed away. Rachel knew that though he was a blessed gift to Israel, she would not live to bring him up. Hopefully, before she died, she heard Jacob renaming their baby Benjamin, 'son of my right hand'.

Rachel's death, combining both great joy and great loss, echoes the lives of all the wives of the patriarchs. It also speaks into today. Generations come and go for us too. Family life is marked with longing and hope, disappointment and fulfilment, birth and death, blessings and sorrow. Yet Christ beckons us on, into service and lives lived in the purposes of God.

We thank you, Lord, that our times are in your hands. We pray that we may use each day in worship of you and service of others. In the name of Christ. Amen

ELAINE STORKEY

What Jesus said in his final hours

Lyndall Bywater writes:

I've never been great with sad stories. I'll willingly skip to the next chapter if the bit of the book I'm reading is proving too upsetting. Perhaps it's because I read for escapism; perhaps it's because I wish life were altogether less sad. Whatever the reason, not liking sad stories makes Easter a complex time for me.

I grew up in a Christian family, so this story of torture and execution has been with me all my life. Granted, it has just about the happiest ending ever, but the majority of it is heartbreakingly painful. That being said, I believe passionately that we Christians need not be afraid to examine the death of Jesus with our minds and hearts, because it is the lynchpin of history and of our own salvation.

For the next two weeks, we will be walking through the 24 hours or so leading up to Jesus' death on the cross. But instead of trying to make sense of the baffling events – the betrayals, the rigged court cases and the trauma of crucifixion – we will be listening to the words Jesus spoke. Perhaps we will identify with some of the emotions he expressed; perhaps we will learn from his wisdom in handling dangerous people; perhaps we will find comfort in the way he never stopped being himself, no matter how much pressure he was under. Above all, though, I hope and pray we will encounter afresh the astonishing truth that he did it for us.

Spending 14 days in a story we would normally read over just one or two days may feel heavy going. I'm the sort of writer who likes to raise a chuckle and there aren't many of those to be had when we're considering the unjust killing of an innocent man. This is a story where tragedy and trauma seem to have the upper hand. If that's what you're living at the moment, there will be much that resonates. If it's not, I encourage you to think about others who might be living that sort of reality: friends or family members who are grieving; people who are being persecuted for their faith; parts of the world where darkness seems to hold sway. And then pray for those people and those places, because this story is the key that opens the door to light, justice, hope and healing.

All of you

Then he took a cup, and after giving thanks he gave it to them, saying, 'Drink from it, all of you; for this is my blood of the covenant, which is poured out for many for the forgiveness of sins.' (NRSV)

What would you choose to do on your last evening of peace before a major ordeal? Perhaps you've been there – finding ways to pass the time the night before taking an exam or going into hospital for an operation. Would you watch a film, go out with friends or just wile away a quiet evening doing as little as possible?

I wonder when Jesus knew this was it. He'd known his life was in danger for a long time, but now the hour had come. Today's reading finds him marking the first meal of Passover, and it certainly feels as though he knew nothing would ever be the same again. It's significant that the place he chose to spend that evening full of foreboding was with his friends, even though they probably had no idea what was just around the corner.

There was a moment during the meal when Jesus used part of the Passover liturgy to express something profound. He shared the wine with them, not as the usual festive ritual but as a covenant, offering the cup as an invitation to be a part of something – something to do with the hope of a new kind of kingdom.

But perhaps the most striking thing about that moment was the fact that Judas and Peter were there, the two who would fail him in the most public ways in the coming hours. He didn't wait for them to leave the room or send them packing. His invitation to drink to a new, hope-filled future was for all of them, not just the ones who would get things right.

'All of you' includes us. That cup is yours too. You may feel you've failed, you may even feel you've betrayed Jesus, but he's still holding that cup out to you.

Each time you have a drink today, stop for a moment and thank Jesus for including you.

LYNDALL BYWATER

You will; I will

Jesus said to him, 'Truly I tell you, this very night, before the cock crows, you will deny me three times.' (NRSV)

I used to commute into London for work. The journey was about two hours each way on a good day. On a bad day, of which there were many, it could be anywhere between two and five! This didn't matter too much for a day in the office, since I could work on the train, but it played havoc with my ability to turn up on time to meetings, particularly if they involved me travelling at rush hour. I quickly learnt to avoid promising, 'I will definitely be there by…'

In today's reading, we happen upon the disciples having a painful conversation with Jesus, a conversation which involves several 'I wills'. Perhaps by now they'd worked out that this wasn't a normal Passover. There was a sense of foreboding, as Jesus spoke about the things to come. Peter, ever one to show up first in a crisis, clearly felt that bold commitments were needed. 'I will never desert you,' he said (v. 33), and it's easy to believe he meant it, but his intentions were nowhere near equal to the trial they were all about to face.

Jesus knew Peter would fail him. Instead of glossing over that truth or sugar-coating it to make it more palatable, he met Peter's 'I will' with a simple, devastating truth: 'You will deny me three times' (v. 34).

Yet Jesus had an 'I will' of his own to offer his friends. 'After I am raised up, I will go ahead of you to Galilee' (v. 32). No matter what happened next, no matter how wrong things went, the disciples were to hold on to the truth that Jesus would return to them.

Our 'I wills' are always tinged with human weakness and the unpredictability of circumstances, but Jesus' 'I will' is solid and unshakable.

God makes thousands of 'I will' promises in scripture. Think of as many as you can and write them down. Which one do you need to hold especially tightly today?

LYNDALL BYWATER

Not what I want

He said, 'Abba, Father, for you all things are possible; remove this cup from me; yet, not what I want, but what you want.' (NRSV)

'Just let go and I'll catch you!' It's the sort of thing they say to you when you're stuck somewhere high up and need to let go, trusting that someone will catch you on the way down. I have no idea how you persuade yourself to let go of the only solid thing in reach and let yourself plummet!

Jesus was on his way to die. How could a loving father countenance such a terrible thing when he had the power to stop it? Was it really the only way? These are important questions, but this isn't the place to explore them. Let's pause for a moment, though, and catch a glimpse of the relationship between the Father and the Son, portrayed so powerfully in today's reading.

Jesus didn't want to die. He believed it was God's plan for him, but there in Gethsemane it's as though the enormity of it finally overwhelmed him, and in that moment, he called out in desperation to his dad. Then he got up and walked the most terrifying journey a human has ever walked. Somewhere in that turning point were the words: 'Not what I want but what you want.' With that simple phrase, he let go and let himself fall, trusting himself to the one who named him 'Beloved Son'.

There are so many different ways to say those words. You could say them dutifully, because you think God expects something from you. You could say them resignedly, because you don't believe what you want matters to God. You could say them grudgingly, because you feel God is asking something of you that's unfair. Or, like Jesus, you could say them in soul-surrendering trust, because you know that the one you say them to loves you completely and wants only the best for you.

Every so often, it's worth taking time to ponder these two questions: Do I really believe God has my best interests at heart? And do I trust God to carry me through the worst that life has to offer?

LYNDALL BYWATER

Willing but weak

Then he came to the disciples and found them sleeping; and he said
to Peter, 'So, could you not stay awake with me one hour? Stay awake
and pray that you may not come into the time of trial; the spirit indeed
is willing, but the flesh is weak.' (NRSV)

A friend and I were once having a conversation about eyesight. He'd just
had new glasses and they weren't quite right. His vision was blurry. The
prescription was wrong. It would cost a lot to get them corrected. I listened
attentively, making sympathetic noises until I could no longer resist the
urge to comment on the irony. You see, I'm blind. I can hardly see a thing.
I'm sure glasses can be the bane of one's life, but I'd give a king's ransom
to be able to see with them, even poorly!

Today finds us in the same story as we read yesterday, though from a
different gospel and it strikes me as another kind of irony. Jesus was in
prayer, facing down the most terrifying ordeal of his life and wondering
how he would find the courage to do what needed to be done. But when he
returned to his disciples, they were fast asleep because even staying awake
for one hour of prayer was too much of an ordeal for them.

I used to read these words about the willing spirit and the weak flesh
and think Jesus was angry, offended or disappointed, but nowadays what
I hear in these words is a gentle empathy. These beloved friends of his were
about to face their own ordeals. Their flesh was about to prove very weak
indeed, and their willing spirits would fail them at the last. Jesus' words
were true for them, but they were truest of all for himself. He knew fragility
better than anyone. It's easy to be hard on ourselves when we feel fragile.
We think we should cope better, work harder, be braver, pray more, but
Jesus knows what it is to be fragile and he meets our fragility with empathy
and kindness.

---

*How kind are you to yourself when you feel fragile? Do you beat yourself up
and push yourself harder or are you able to lean back into the kindness of
Jesus? Next time life feels like an ordeal, how might you be kinder to yourself?*

LYNDALL BYWATER

Put your sword back

Then Jesus said to him, 'Put your sword back into its place; for all who take the sword will perish by the sword. Do you think that I cannot appeal to my Father, and he will at once send me more than twelve legions of angels?' (NRSV)

I like to think of myself as a gentle, peace-loving soul, but the one thing guaranteed to get me riled up is my computer. It only has to do something unexpected, fail to do something perfectly logical or just start running slowly and I'm ready to reach for the sledgehammer. It's illogical of course – smashing the thing up will only land me in even more strife – but it's surprising how tempting the urge can be.

To use a computing term, one of the shortcuts we humans have acquired is to react aggressively when we feel frustrated or endangered. When Peter saw a mob with weapons bearing down on his band of friends, something boiled over inside him and he lashed out with his sword, leaving one of the high priest's servants without an ear.

Psychologists understand that aggression urge is a protective response, designed to keep us safe when we're in danger from anyone or anything that might intend to harm us. Theologians might add the idea that it's part of our sinful nature. Whichever it is, it's interesting to note that Jesus sidestepped it. Being as human as you or me, he may well have felt the urge to protect himself in that moment of imminent personal danger, but he chose not to let aggression take over. Instead, he kept doing what he had come to do. He healed.

There are times to fight against injustice, but the aggression that surges in me when I'm thwarted or wounded rarely brings justice. It usually comes out in sharp words or passive aggressive silences, neither of which help or heal. Jesus invites us to put away our swords, not because our feelings don't matter but because there's something bigger going on and he wants us to trust him in it.

Jesus, forgive me when my aggressive responses have wounded others. In those hot-headed moments, help me hear your calming voice, trust you and find wiser ways to work towards justice. Amen

LYNDALL BYWATER

You have said so but...

But Jesus was silent. Then the high priest said to him, 'I put you under oath... tell us if you are the Messiah, the Son of God.' Jesus said to him, 'You have said so. But I tell you, from now on you will see the Son of Man seated at the right hand of Power and coming on the clouds of heaven.' (NRSV)

There can be few things more unpleasant than listening to yourself being lied about. Perhaps you've had that experience: being accused of something you haven't done, becoming the subject of gossip or finding yourself misunderstood. The truth is we're created for connection and relationship, so it matters that people know us and think the best of us.

Jesus was in court, facing a barrage of accusations about what he had, and hadn't, said and done. What's more, his accusers had lined up false witnesses to make up stories about him, just to add weight to the lies. For the most part, he remained silent, but eventually the high priest put him on oath and he was obliged to say something.

I confess I find his words baffling. He seemed to make things worse for himself. Why couldn't he have dismantled the prosecution's case point by point? Instead, refusing to play their game, he chose to say something about his own deepest truth and his own future hope.

He spoke of the Son of Man sitting at the right hand of power. In the face of falsehoods and wilful misunderstandings, there must have been some comfort in the truth that he would soon sit side by side with the Father who called him beloved. And he spoke of a day when God would come to his people in a way that all would see and recognise. As he watched his disciples disperse and his ministry seemingly crumble, that reminder of the coming kingdom must have given him hope.

Are people saying untrue things about you? Sometimes we can defend ourselves. Sometimes we can't. But we can always speak words of deep truth and future hope over ourselves.

Is there a deep truth that brings you comfort? Is there a promise from God that gives you hope for the future? Hold these in mind and speak them to yourself when others seem to have got you all wrong.

LYNDALL BYWATER

For this I came into the world

Pilate asked him, 'So you are a king?' Jesus answered, 'You say that I am a king. For this I was born, and for this I came into the world, to testify to the truth. Everyone who belongs to the truth listens to my voice.' (NRSV)

I once worked in a large office block where we had drinks-making areas scattered throughout the building… and then the powers that be banned kettles! I won't regale you with the many tales of civil unrest and clandestine kettle-boiling; suffice it to say, workplace politics was turbulent for quite some time.

Much of what happened to Jesus in the time leading up to his death was about politics, and this interview with Pilate is no exception. Pilate seems to have been a more open-minded audience than the religious court we visited yesterday. He had questions about who Jesus was, why the religious authorities had taken issue with him and even about the nature of truth itself. For his part, Jesus seems to have been more willing to answer, though he still wouldn't let himself be drawn into the question of whether he claimed to be a king, perhaps because he knew something of the politics going on between Rome and Jerusalem.

The worst kind of politics is the kind that puts systems, rules and policies ahead of people; the kind that plays a game to win, no matter who gets hurt along the way. Jesus was in the grip of that kind of politics as he talked with Pilate, and Jesus' words give us a helpful steer for those awkward moments when we get caught up in 'politics' at work, at home or at church.

'For this I came.' As powerful forces quarrelled over his identity and vied for his life, Jesus spoke a simple affirmation of why he was alive. Next time you feel like you're caught up in politics, step back from the gameplay and look for what's most important. Remind yourself of what God has called you to be and to do in that place.

Jesus, revealer of truth, give me clear sight to see things as they are. Help me look out for those being harmed by political gameplay. Help me hold on to my God-given identity, no matter what conflict happens around me. Amen
LYNDALL BYWATER

Weep

But Jesus turned to them and said, 'Daughters of Jerusalem, do not weep for me, but weep for yourselves and for your children.' (NRSV)

Over the past few years, I've found myself in prayer meetings where we've sensed God's call to lament. Lament is all about speaking out in prayer how bad things have got. That sounds easy, doesn't it, but it really isn't. We're hardwired to want to speak hope, so there's an almost irresistible urge to end our prayers with, 'But we know it'll all be alright in the end.' There's nothing wrong with speaking hope, of course, but there's something important (and biblical) about daring to sit in the darkness without putting the lights on straight away.

Jesus didn't walk towards his crucifixion proclaiming his resurrection. He had told his disciples that he would rise from the dead, which suggests he knew the Father might have a radical plan for hope, but he didn't ever mention that on the way to his death. Instead, his words were laden with lament. When he spotted the women weeping, he didn't tell them to cheer up and put their faith in God for better days ahead. He encouraged them to weep at the sheer awfulness of what was happening.

While the women wept, another person entered the story. Simon of Cyrene stepped in to carry the cross. In a typical goody-vs-baddy film, Simon might be the one who grabs the cross and helps Jesus fight his way out to freedom, but in the Bible Simon just carried the cross. Even Jesus needed someone to stay with him and help him carry the terrible heaviness of it all.

It's an art to sit in lament, and it's an art to sit in lament with someone else – to resist solving things for them and instead to help them carry their cross. It's an art our world needs the church to learn.

Is there someone who needs you to sit with them in sorrow today? Could you visit or simply get in contact to let them know you're thinking of them, praying for them and grieving with them?

LYNDALL BYWATER

They do not know

Then Jesus said, 'Father, forgive them; for they do not know what they are doing.' (NRSV)

Are you any good at complaining? I don't mean grumbling about life in general; I mean making a complaint to a company about poor service or a substandard product. I find it intensely awkward. I think that's because I'm pouring out my frustration to someone on the end of a phone or across a counter, yet the thing I'm complaining about invariably isn't their fault. I worry about them taking the brunt of my displeasure when the real culprit is probably a defective system or a policy they have no control over.

Today's reading brings us to the moment of Jesus' crucifixion. The politicians have had their day in court, the religious leaders have got what they wanted and now Jesus is in the hands of the soldiers, the ordinary blokes who had to action the decisions made by those in power. And it's for these men that Jesus has words of forgiveness. We presume that the one who was 'full of grace and truth' (John 1:14) forgave all those who had a part in his death, but he spoke that forgiveness out loud over those soldiers.

They were by no means innocent. They had mocked him and insulted him throughout, and they continued even when he was on the cross, but it's as though Jesus wanted to make the distinction that they weren't culpable in the same way. They were conscripted to participate in a story they neither chose nor understood.

Injustice is never easy to handle. Whether it's being overcharged for something, being treated unfairly at work or being hurt by a friend, it can help to take a step back and consider what's really going on. Chances are we will still need to forgive but getting perspective on the situation can make that forgiving a little easier.

Lord, I confess that being treated unfairly can bring out the worst in me. Forgive me when I lash out at those around me instead of leaning into you. Help me to see what you want me to see. Amen

LYNDALL BYWATER

You will be with me in paradise

**He replied, 'Truly I tell you, today you will be with me in Paradise.'
(NRSV)**

They say being under pressure brings out what is deepest in us. We do what comes most naturally to us, we do what matters most to us – whether it's the parent who finds superhuman strength to keep caring for a child when they themselves are seriously ill, the emergency services worker who keeps rescuing people from danger long after their own physical resources have run out or the person on the hospital ward who's still making everyone laugh despite their own pain.

Today's reading is another glimpse of those last hours of Jesus' life. There on the cross, in the grip of unbearable agony, no one would have blamed him if he'd shut out everything and everyone around him, focusing all his resources on dealing with the trauma in his body; no one would have blamed him if he'd ranted at the injustice of the situation; no one would have blamed him if he'd flung some words of rebuke at the criminal who jeered at him. Instead, he reached beyond his own pain and did the thing which came most naturally to him: he brought hope to another human being.

He'd been doing it for years – hearing the cries of those who were bound up in sorrow, sickness and oppression, turning his attention towards them and helping them find wholeness in mind and body – and here, in the final moments before death overtook him, he did it again. Even then, love poured out of him.

This is our God. No matter how dark things get, God's heart is always to enfold us in love and reach us with salvation. And this is our God's invitation to us: to be those who instinctively bring love and hope, wherever we find ourselves.

Fill a sponge with water and squeeze it. We humans are like sponges: when squeezed, we pour out what's been poured in. Do you make space to be with God and to be filled up with love and hope?

LYNDALL BYWATER

Here is your blessing

When Jesus saw his mother and the disciple whom he loved standing beside her, he said to his mother, 'Woman, here is your son.' Then he said to the disciple, 'Here is your mother.' And from that hour the disciple took her into his own home. (NRSV)

American author Napoleon Hill's book *Think and Grow Rich* (The Ralston Society, 1937) is one of the top ten bestselling self-help books of all time. In it he wrote: 'Every adversity, every failure, and every heartache, carries with it the seed of an equivalent or greater benefit.'

Today's passage finds us again standing near the cross, watching a tragedy unfold. It's not easy to linger here, is it? Yet there are glimmers of grace among the shadows.

The gospel accounts tell us that most of Jesus' followers had fled by the time he was crucified. There were very few friendly faces in the crowd around him in those darkest of hours, but there were two people whom he held very dear. His mum was there – the woman who had been warned, just a few days after his birth, that a sword would pierce her soul on account of him (Luke 2:35) – and one of his disciples, called 'the Beloved'. They hadn't let the horror of it all drive them away. They had decided to stick with him and because they were present in that moment, they received a blessing which would stay with them for the rest of their lives. Mary, who was probably a widow by this point, got a home and family, and John got the gift of a mother.

Yesterday's passage reminded us that it is the unchanging nature of God to bring people hope and salvation. Today we're reminded that it is the nature of God to use tragedy to disperse seeds of blessing. None of us would choose to go through tragedy. In fact, we do all we can to avoid it. But if we can find the courage to be present in the pain, just as John and Mary were, we find unexpected blessings poured out on us.

What unexpected blessings have you received as a direct result of going through tough times? When you think about the things you're most grateful for in life, how many of them have come out of difficulty or struggle?

LYNDALL BYWATER

My God, why?

And about three o'clock Jesus cried with a loud voice, 'Eli, Eli, lema sabachthani?' that is, 'My God, my God, why have you forsaken me?' (NRSV)

Do you ever have 'jukebox days', or is it just me? A jukebox day is one where everything people say to you seems to bring a song to mind. A passing comment that it's raining has you humming Buddy Holly, or a simple 'hello' has you breaking into a U2 song. (Which of these two you most relate to may say something about how old you are.) It's evidence, if ever we needed it, that the songs we know best sink deep into the fabric of our brains and spring spontaneously to mind at the slightest provocation.

Today's passage is another account of Jesus on the cross, and one which brings us perhaps the bleakest moment of that utterly bleak event. Jesus, beloved Son, intimately close to the Father in all things, uttered desolate words of rejection and abandonment. These weren't just any old words though. These were words of a song which would have been nestled deep in his brain, thanks to years and years of singing it (Psalm 22:1). As the life slowly left his body, those familiar words came to his aid, helping him to express his despair.

How much of the Bible have you sunk into your brain? Are there verses which come to mind readily when you need them? If you're anything like me, it may never have occurred to you to memorise a verse like this one from Psalm 22. We tend to prefer to commit upbeat, hopeful verses to memory. But the Bible has far more to offer. It contains every colour of human emotion. We talked a few days ago about the importance of lament, but do we hold verses of lament in our minds so that they can come to our aid when we need words for our pain?

One of the best ways to sink the Bible into your brain is to sing it. Look for songs which set scripture to music or write your own. That way, your jukebox days will be full of God's words.

LYNDALL BYWATER

Into your hands

Then Jesus, crying with a loud voice, said, 'Father, into your hands I commend my spirit.' Having said this, he breathed his last. (NRSV)

Creazione di Adamo is one of the fresco paintings by Michelangelo on the ceiling of the Sistine Chapel. Central to the image are two hands – one Adam's, reaching up towards God, and the other God's, reaching down towards Adam. God's finger is outstretched, ready to impart the spark of life.

It's Good Friday, the day when we remember Jesus, the second Adam, who surrendered his life to overturn the curses of sin and death. In some small way we have accompanied him on his journey by reading his story and now we reach his very last moments of life. We've listened to his words: his farewells to his friends; his resolute refusal to play political games in the courts; and his outpouring of forgiveness, grace and love, even while nailed to a cross. Yesterday we caught the strains of a song of despair, the cry of one who felt himself abandoned by God, and today we hear his final words. Given that feeling of abandonment, it would be understandable if those words had a ring of bitterness. Indeed, we might even have thought that God really had abandoned his Son. But these final words ring not with bitterness but with trust. They're not words of turning away but of turning towards. 'Into your hands…' Somewhere deep in the torment, deeper still than the fear of separation from his Father, Jesus knew those same hands were outstretched to receive him. The hands that sparked life would cradle his spirit at the point of death.

The hands of God hold you today. They spark life where you feel dead inside. They hold you up when you feel weak and fragile. They will catch you and cradle you when you fall. You can entrust yourself fully into those hands.

Father, into your hands I commend my life. Into your hands I commend my hopes, my fears, my sorrows and my joys. Into your hands I commend myself, trusting that you will sustain me and bring me to new life. Amen

LYNDALL BYWATER

I confer on you a kingdom

'You are those who have stood by me in my trials; and I confer on you, just as my Father has conferred on me, a kingdom.' (NRSV)

How do you get on with non-linear timelines? A book or film is non-linear when the scenes occur out of sequence and the plot line jumps forwards and backwards in time. I'm okay with a few flashbacks and flashforwards, but my brain scrambles when I can't track how it all fits together.

For this final day of our two weeks of listening to the words of Jesus, we find ourselves back in scene one. We're back at the dinner table where the bread was eaten and the cup of covenant was drunk, and the horrors of the hours to come are still a future possibility. Yet Jesus seems to be doing a bit of a flashforward, telling his disciples that they will stand with him through all that's about to happen and that they will inherit something of great worth.

These words are even more remarkable for the fact that, for the most part, they didn't stand with him. They fled, they lied and they disowned him. He knew they would, yet he willingly forgave, even before the wrongs were done and spoke promise into their future.

That promise was a kingdom, and the journey we've just walked gives us a few hints as to what that kingdom is like. It's a world where everyone can drink the cup of welcome, where our failings are covered by grace and where our fragility is embraced by kindness. It's a world where we know who we are in God and we don't have to get caught up in political gameplay, and where we can be honest about grief and injustice. It's a world where healing, forgiveness and grace spring up, even in the darkest moments. And it's a world where we can entrust ourselves to the everlasting arms of God's love.

'There's a wideness in God's mercy… There's a kindness in God's justice… For the love of God is broader than the measures of the mind, and the heart of the Eternal is most wonderfully kind.' (Frederick William Faber, 1814–63).

LYNDALL BYWATER

Igniting hope

Catherine Butcher writes:

What do you hope for? Better health? Improved relationships? Financial security? Ultimately, the hope that Christians have focuses on the events of Easter. The whole Bible pivots on the three days when Jesus was crucified, died and was buried, then rose again from the dead.

When the relationship between God and humanity was broken, as described in Genesis, all of creation looked forward to the day when God would repair that brokenness. Jesus bridged the gap between us and God when he died on the cross. Then, in the 40 days between the resurrection and the ascension, Jesus appeared to hundreds of people. Hope was ignited, and now that Jesus has returned to his Father, we live looking forward to the day when Jesus will return to make all things new.

Once the reality of Jesus' resurrection dawned on the first disciples, they went on to share their new-found hope throughout Jerusalem, Judea and to the ends of the earth. That hope, ignited by God's Holy Spirit, stood the test of time and gave them the strength to withstand persecution. Some were martyred because they refused to deny their faith.

Over the next two weeks, we will be looking at those first people whose hope was ignited by meeting Jesus in the 40 days after his resurrection. Those women and men went on to ignite hope in others, and the flame of hope kindled in them still burns today as we too become people of hope.

This is not an inherited hope. Just like the first disciples, hope is ignited in us as we meet the risen Christ for ourselves. As he said, 'Blessed are those who have not seen [me] and yet have believed' (John 20:29, NIV).

In the last five days of our focus on hope, we will look at five different ways in which we can be people who bring hope into the world: evangelism, discipleship, service, seeking justice and caring for our world.

I trust that these studies will ignite hope in your life and inspire you to bring hope into every context and situation you face. I am praying that, over this fortnight, you will encounter Jesus afresh and be changed by the power of his love.

Look out for the 'Alive' video course produced by HOPE Together and KingsGate Community Church, due out by this Easter, which also focuses on the post-resurrection appearances of Jesus.

A glimmer of hope

'You are looking for Jesus the Nazarene, who was crucified. He has risen! He is not here.' (NIV)

Celebrity cook Mary Berry found that it was her Christian faith that sustained her when her 19-year-old son was killed in a car crash. Following the tragedy she said, 'William's death deepened my faith; without its support, I really would have struggled.'

When someone close dies, it's hard to come to terms with the loss. Maybe it was just a bad dream. But for Jesus' first-century followers, his death was all too real. They had watched his agonising crucifixion. They knew his body had been buried hurriedly in a borrowed tomb.

Then suddenly, the tomb was empty. Their emotions were thrown into reverse. No wonder the women were 'trembling and bewildered'. Could they believe what they were seeing? Was this a glimmer of hope?

The women had gone to the tomb, hoping to give Jesus' body a proper burial. Now they were racking their brains to rethink everything they had seen and heard. They had watched Jesus healing people from diseases, casting out demons and even raising people from the dead. Could he have overcome death itself? Could he possibly be alive again?

They had heard him talk about laying down his life for the sheep… and taking it up again (John 10:17). Mark even wrote: '"The Son of Man is going to be delivered into the hands of men. They will kill him, and after three days he will rise." But they did not understand what he meant and were afraid to ask him about it' (Mark 9:31–32).

For those women – and for each of us – everything changed on that first Easter Day. Now we have hope that lasts beyond the grave. It makes all the difference, even in the saddest times.

What difference does Jesus' resurrection mean for you today?

Give thanks for Jesus' death and resurrection. Especially if you are afraid of dying, ask God to light a fresh flame of hope in your heart and to overwhelm you with his love.

CATHERINE BUTCHER

113

First witnesses

They remembered his words. When they came back from the tomb, they told all these things to the Eleven and to all the others. (NIV)

The resurrection seemed unbelievable, especially when the reports came from women. In Jesus' time a woman's testimony was not admissible in court. And that makes the gospel accounts all the more believable. If the resurrection was just fiction, written to convince people of a lie, no sensible author would make women the first witnesses of Jesus' resurrection.

The fact of Jesus' resurrection gives us an amazing hope – hope that the man we read of in the gospels is real and can be known; hope that, because of him, we can receive God's gift of abundant life now and for the future.

It also gives particular hope to women worldwide. In the UK, equal rights for women have been hard won, though not always achieved in practice. In many parts of the world, women are still second-class citizens or treated as servants.

But, as Paul reminded us, in Christ 'there is neither Jew nor Gentile, neither slave nor free, nor is there male and female, for you are all one in Christ Jesus' (Galatians 3:28).

Jesus elevated the status of women and often meets us as we go about our daily tasks. The women in our reading today were preparing to embalm a body. Jesus also met a woman fetching water from a well; he met Martha and Mary when they were mourning the death of Lazarus.

In each encounter he brings hope, hope that we can pass on to others.

Where will you meet with Jesus today? Who needs you to pass on the hope you have to them? What words of scripture have spoken to you in the past? What promises from God do you need to remember today?

Invite God to meet you in your everyday tasks today, perhaps using the prayer of St Richard of Chichester: 'To see you more clearly, love you more dearly, follow you more nearly, day by day.'

CATHERINE BUTCHER

A lightbulb moment

Finally the other disciple, who had reached the tomb first, also went inside. He saw and believed. (NIV)

When did you first realise that God loves you? For some it is a gradual realisation. For others God's love is like a bolt of lightning.

John's gospel points out that it was still dark when Mary Magdalene arrived at the empty tomb; physically dark before sunrise and spiritually dark before it dawned on her that Jesus was alive. Her first response was to run to tell Simon Peter and John, 'the disciple Jesus loved'. They raced to the tomb and John hesitated before going in. Then he saw the grave clothes lying like an empty chrysalis, with the cloth that had been wrapped round Jesus' head lying separate from the rest of the linen. That's when John believed that Jesus was the Son of God.

John's life changed forever and, in the years that followed, he allowed that lightbulb moment to reinterpret everything he had heard from Jesus. As Jesus had asked John to care for Mary, Jesus' mother, John must have spent time with her talking through all that she pondered in her heart (Luke 2:19). Together, their reflections gave John a special understanding of the hope we have.

John's gospel was the last of the four accounts of Jesus' life to be written. It is quite different from the other three, drawing out themes and highlighting aspects of Jesus' life to prove conclusively that God loved the world so much that he gave his one and only Son so that we can have eternal life (John 3:16).

Light and darkness are among John's key themes. It is John who records Jesus' promise: 'I am the light of the world. Whoever follows me will never walk in darkness, but will have the light of life' (John 8:12).

Where are the dark places in your life or in the lives of those around you? Invite Jesus into these places. Ask God to use you to bring his light and hope into the lives of others today.

CATHERINE BUTCHER

Despair becomes hope

He asked her, 'Woman, why are you crying? Who is it you are looking for?' (NIV)

Mary Magdalene's passionate pursuit of Jesus brought a special reward. She was among the women who set off for the tomb as soon as the Sabbath rest was over. When they found the tomb empty, Mary was distraught. She didn't realise he had risen from the dead and was determined to find his body. Blinded by her tears. Overcome with grief. That's when she heard his voice. And then he called her name.

Notice the tenderness of that moment when Mary is the first person on the planet to meet the risen Christ. It marks a turning point in her relationship with Jesus. She is not to cling to him. Instead, she is told to go and tell the others that Jesus is alive.

Moments of personal encounter with Jesus are precious and often lead to a fresh commission.

My personal stand-out moment took place on a Sunday morning service when one of the church leaders brought a prophetic word for me about God using my writing nationally. I was training as a journalist but had failed English A-level first time round. Who'd have thought I'd make a career out of writing? Forty years later and I can see that God has been true to that word.

What moments stand out for you in your journey with Jesus? Are there Bible characters whose lives are a particular inspiration to you? Are there verses of scripture which God seems to have underlined for you?

We don't all receive a unique call from God but, like Mary Magdalene, we are all called to be the unique person God has made us in the places he puts us. We are all called to be Jesus' followers and to pass on the hope he gives us.

Read Isaiah 43:1–4 and allow these ancient words to speak to you today as Jesus calls you by name and commissions you to bring hope to others: 'You are mine… I will be with you… you are precious… and… I love you.'

CATHERINE BUTCHER

A post-resurrection rethink

And beginning with Moses and all the Prophets, he explained to them what was said in all the scriptures concerning himself. (NIV)

About 20 years ago my Christian life had become dry. It was all work (I work mainly for Christian charities writing about faith). In that desert place I read a book that prompted me to rethink my relationship with Jesus. As I read *The Sacred Romance: Drawing closer to the heart of God* by Brent Curtis and John Eldredge (Thomas Nelson, 1997), I realised that the films, poetry, songs and stories that most stirred my heart were simply echoes of an epic love story: God's rescue plan for humanity. My first love for Jesus was reignited as I saw the Bible in a fresh light: a story of adventure, risk, betrayal, loss and heroism. I was caught up again in the great romance between Christ and his church.

I'd love to have been with the duo on the road to Emmaus as Jesus unpacked scripture for them. The couple were not among the twelve disciples. They might have seen Jesus give thanks and break the loaves when he fed 5,000 people (Mark 6:41) or they might have been at the last supper. Watching Jesus break bread in their home was their turning point. Cleopas, who is named by Luke, might be the same person as Clopas (John 19:25) who was married to Mary, one of the witnesses to the crucifixion. She was possibly the same Mary described as the mother of James (Luke 24:10), who went to the tomb on that first Easter Sunday.

Whatever their identity, they had been told that Jesus was alive. They would have known what prophets like Isaiah and Jeremiah had said about the coming Messiah. And their hearts were 'burning' as he walked and talked with them. But they still did not believe.

Hope was ignited in their hearts when they recognised Jesus. They couldn't wait to spread the good news.

Do you need to take a fresh look at Jesus? Ask him to open your heart so you rediscover his love for you. Invite him to show you who else needs to hear the good news of God's love.

CATHERINE BUTCHER

God's rescue plan

He said to them, 'This is what I told you while I was still with you: everything must be fulfilled that is written about me in the Law of Moses, the Prophets and the Psalms.' (NIV)

A classic structure for epic stories starts with harmony. That harmony is then disturbed, but a hero is found. The hero accepts the quest to restore what has been lost. There are tests and trials to overcome, but finally harmony is restored. Think of your favourite stories and their heroes. Do they fit this structure? What about heroes like Bilbo Baggins, Harry Potter, Jo March, Luke Skywalker, to name but a few?

Like the disciples we can often feel troubled and full of doubts. It's as if we find ourselves in the middle of a story that can be wonderful but is often confusing and sometimes tragic. How can we make sense of our story?

The disciples had watched Jesus riding into Jerusalem on a donkey, heralded by crowds shouting 'Hosanna'. It must have seemed like a high point, the pinnacle of their journey with Jesus. Was he now going to rescue the Jewish nation from their Roman oppressors, restoring all they had lost? Their hopes were dashed when he was tried and sent to the cross. How could he be their hero now?

When Jesus appeared to the disciples, he gave them fresh hope. He was physically present with them. They could touch him. They watched him eat. Although he had mysteriously appeared in their midst, he was not a ghost. And as he 'opened their minds so they could understand the scriptures' he put himself into the context of all of history.

Hope is ignited when we see ourselves as part of God's rescue plan for humanity. After that encounter with Jesus, his disciples were inspired to live heroic lives, empowered by God's Holy Spirit to take the gospel to the ends of the earth. You too have a part to play in God's rescue plan.

Have you overlooked the Old Testament? Maybe you find hope in the psalms, but what about Moses' law and the prophets? Ask God to help you to appreciate all of scripture as a source of hope.

CATHERINE BUTCHER

Doubt defeated

He said to Thomas, 'Put your finger here; see my hands. Reach out your hand and put it into my side. Stop doubting and believe.' Thomas said to him, 'My Lord and my God!' (NIV)

When an elderly patient shared her faith with Dr Francis Collins, she then asked him what he believed. Although he was a scientist (he oversaw the Human Genome Project's 15-year effort to map and sequence human DNA), he had never looked at the evidence for Jesus. When he began to find out about Jesus he said, 'Here was a person with remarkably strong evidence for his life, who made astonishing statements about loving your neighbour and whose claims about being God's son seemed to demand a decision.'

Two years after that conversation at a patient's bedside, after 'kicking and screaming most of the way,' Dr Collins made the decision to become a Christian and has since discovered 'science can actually be a means of worship'.

In our reading today Thomas also wanted evidence that Jesus was alive. He wasn't prepared to accept what the other disciples had to say. He wanted to see Jesus for himself.

He had a questioning mind. Earlier in John's gospel we read that Thomas asked Jesus: 'Lord, we don't know where you are going, so how can we know the way?' (John 14:5).

Jesus deals gently with him. He knows what Thomas had said when he refused to believe he was alive, so he invites Thomas to touch the wounds in his hands and side.

Thomas responds immediately to Jesus' command to 'stop doubting and believe', exclaiming, 'My Lord and my God!' In doing so, he annoucnes that the Jesus he had followed, was also the God he worshipped.

The hope ignited in Thomas' heart that day continued to energise him for the rest of his life as he took the good news of the risen Christ to India, where he was martyred for his faith.

Everyone has doubts at times. Sometimes we need to go back to basics and re-examine the evidence for our faith. Often, we need a fresh encounter with Jesus to reignite hope. Ask God to speak to you afresh today.

CATHERINE BUTCHER

Sure and certain hope

Jesus came, took the bread and gave it to them, and did the same with the fish. This was now the third time Jesus appeared to his disciples after he was raised from the dead. (NIV)

Hosting or helping with Alpha courses has become a regular feature of life for me over the past decade. During the Covid-19 lockdowns we ran Alpha online. An online Alpha suits some people better than the in-person alternative: they don't have to arrange childcare; there's no need to worry about access issues; the course can be enjoyed from the familiar comfort of their own home. But I do enjoy getting together face-to-face with the groups to eat and chat together. Sharing a meal often seems to put people at ease, and strong friendships are more easily formed. It is wonderful to see a group of sceptical strangers becoming friends, exploring faith and some then putting their trust in Jesus and being baptised.

When Jesus met these seven disciples on the beach for breakfast, he had an important lesson to teach about failure. Perhaps the meal was to put them at their ease.

Simon Peter and Zebedee's sons, James and John, were experienced fishermen, but had caught nothing all night. The men must have been tired and disappointed. They had failed, but Jesus was ready to meet their practical, physical needs as well as meeting their need for fresh hope. Just like newcomers on an Alpha course, at first, they didn't recognise Jesus. Then, when they had caught a net full of fish, John was the first to recognise his Lord.

It is important to note that Jesus was seen by groups of the disciples on three occasions. He was not the product of an individual's grief-stricken imagination. He really had risen from the dead.

Jesus' resurrection gives us the sure and certain hope that death has been defeated. We can trust him with our lives now and in eternity because he is who he said he is: the resurrection and the life (John 11:25).

Do you have a small group of friends or a prayer triplet where you can be encouraged and encourage others? Take time today to pray for yourself and others, that you might recognise Jesus at work in your world.

CATHERINE BUTCHER

Love restores

When they had finished eating, Jesus said to Simon Peter, 'Simon son of John, do you love me more than these?' (NIV)

We live by the sea and one summer our family joined a local sailing club. But we soon realised that our other weekend commitments meant that club membership wasn't for us. I had started learning to sail, but I couldn't attend lessons regularly enough. The last straw was the morning the group set off, each in a dingy, to sail across the bay. I hadn't learned enough to cope with the tide, waves, rudder and sails. I had to be towed back to land. That was my last solo sailing trip.

Almost everyone knows what it is like to fail – whether it's failed exams, failed relationships or failure in another sphere of life. Failure can destroy our hopes for the future.

Simon Peter had failed to be faithful to Jesus. While Jesus was facing his accusers before his crucifixion, Peter was warming himself by a fire. As Jesus had predicted, Peter denied knowing Jesus three times.

Today's reading is the first recorded conversation between Jesus and Peter after that denial. Already that morning Peter has failed as a fisherman. Then, when they were eating breakfast by the fire, Jesus asks three questions, using Peter's old name, Simon, rather than Peter – 'the rock'.

Notice Jesus doesn't accuse. His simple questions invite Peter to face up to his failure and to reaffirm his love for his Lord. That's what Peter needed to be restored and recommissioned.

Earlier in John's gospel we read that God loves us and 'did not send his Son into the world to condemn the world, but to save the world' (John 3:17). It is God's love that reaches out to us to restore us when we fail.

Are there areas of your life where you have failed, where Jesus can bring restoration?

Bring to God any areas in your life where you feel you have failed. Say sorry where you need forgiveness, and ask him to reignite hope, restoring and recommissioning you.

CATHERINE BUTCHER

Live as witnesses to Jesus

'You will receive power when the Holy Spirit comes on you; and you will be my witnesses in Jerusalem, and in all Judea and Samaria, and to the ends of the earth.' (NIV)

I trained as a journalist on a local newspaper because I wanted to know how to write about Jesus in newspaper-speak rather than Christian jargon. Over 10 years working for HOPE Together I was privileged to write lots of magazines and books, designed to be given away to people exploring faith. I was thrilled when I heard how they were used.

One lady wrote in a few months after her husband died. She said that she had delivered a copy of *Hope in Uncertain Times* (Biblica, 2020), one of my small booklets, to every home in her village, with a note to explain that she was doing this in memory of her husband. His Christian faith had sustained him, and she wanted others to know that Jesus could give them hope. She was passing on the hope she had to others.

As Christians, we are all witnesses to Jesus and the hope he gives. Some opt for overt ways of sharing that hope; others are less conspicuous. But, as soon as others know we are Jesus' followers, we are being his witnesses, even if we don't realise it.

We are not alone in this. The Holy Spirit goes ahead of us, preparing hearts to receive the hope Jesus gives. He also empowers us, prompting our actions and giving us the right words to say.

In the 40 days from the resurrection to the ascension, the disciples were directionless. As we have seen over the past few days, ten gathered in a locked room; two headed home; seven went back to fishing. When Jesus met them, he gave them fresh hope, which either prompted or commissioned each of them to tell others.

Let's take Jesus at his word, allowing the Holy Spirit to work in and through us to bring hope to others.

Spend some time thinking about the different people you meet in an average week, especially those who don't yet know Jesus. Ask God to fill you with his Holy Spirit, equipping you to be an effective witness to Jesus.

CATHERINE BUTCHER

Make disciples

'Go and make disciples of all nations, baptising them in the name of the Father and of the Son and of the Holy Spirit, and teaching them to obey everything I have commanded you.' (NIV)

As I've said, helping people on their faith journey by running Alpha courses is exciting. Seeing the love of Jesus changing lives is thrilling. But a short course is only the beginning. The best thrill is to see those people declaring their new-found faith in baptism, then walking with them as they get to know Jesus more and become an active part of the local church.

One particular Alpha group stands out. Four years after the course finished, like the disciples, they now worship Jesus, though they still have doubts.

Staying together as a group has made all the difference. They have supported each other through joys and sorrows; weddings and funerals; health and illness. Several of the group were baptised in the sea the summer after the course ended. They've got involved in the life of the church and are actively supporting others on their faith journeys. As new disciples, they are learning to make disciples of others.

This great commission, as these verses are known, is a challenge for us as churches; we each have a part to play. Some are good at standing up front, preaching or teaching; others are gifted in getting alongside people one-to-one; some are practical – good at arranging events or catering; others are great group leaders, drawing out discussion and helping everyone to grow in faith.

Jesus had pulled together a motley crew of disciples, each with different strengths. In those 40 days between the resurrection and the ascension, they seem to have spent a lot of time together. As Jesus appeared to them, their hope grew and became a firm faith once they received the Holy Spirit at Pentecost. Then they were scattered, taking the good news to all nations, held secure, as we are, by Jesus' promise: 'I am with you always.'

Pray today, thanking God for your church and asking where you can play your part in bringing the hope of the gospel to others, especially new believers.

CATHERINE BUTCHER

Put faith into action

'I was hungry and you gave me something to eat, I was thirsty and you gave me something to drink, I was a stranger and you invited me in, I needed clothes and you clothed me…' (NIV)

In March 2020, when church buildings were suddenly forced to close at the start of the Covid-19 crisis, some thought that the church had disappeared. Instead, many churches showed that they were at the heart of their communities as they got involved in shopping, prescription collection, befriending, delivering food packs, making meals, running well-being courses, offering telephone prayer ministry and much more.

Salisbury Cathedral was one of the many historic places of worship which became a vaccine clinic. Some churches became storage depots for food bank supplies. As Caroline Dinenage MP said, '[Churches] are primarily places of worship and yet they also provide refuge during tough times… They are often the first to coordinate charity relief and can often provide meaningful contacts for the lonely and isolated. This has all been especially true during the coronavirus pandemic.'

Alongside evangelism and making disciples, our role as people of hope is to respond together to human need by offering loving service. Today's reading might suggest that our good deeds give us access to heaven. But notice that 'the righteous' in Jesus' story were surprised that their deeds had an impact on Jesus. Reading this story alongside the rest of scripture suggests that as we follow Jesus our response is to serve as he served and to love as he loved, putting others first. The starting point for a life of service is awareness of how much God loves us just as we are. Our service is a response to that amazing truth.

Our actions speak loudly. As the apostle James wrote: 'a person is considered righteous by what they do and not by faith alone' (James 2:24). Let's be people who are known by the way we love others in practical ways, bringing hope to people who are in need.

Words credited to Mother Teresa are: 'The good you do today will often be forgotten. Do good anyway.' Ask God to give you opportunities today to make a positive difference to the lives of others.

CATHERINE BUTCHER

Campaign for justice

'The Spirit of the Lord is on me, because he has anointed me to proclaim good news to the poor... to proclaim freedom for the prisoners and recovery of sight for the blind, to set the oppressed free...' (NIV)

The Trussell Trust was founded in 1997 by Paddy and Carol Henderson from Salisbury, who were working with street children in Bulgaria. The couple's work spread to the UK after Paddy received a call from a mother in Salisbury saying: 'My children are going to bed hungry tonight – what are you going to do about it?'

After researching the issue of short-term hunger in the area, Paddy founded the first of the trust's food banks in the garage and shed of his Salisbury home. In 2004, the UK Foodbank Network was launched, partnering with churches and organisations nationwide who wanted to respond to the need they saw in their communities.

But, as the Trussell Trust says, it takes more than food to end hunger. The trust is using its experience to challenge the structural economic issues that lock people in poverty, and it is campaigning for change to end hunger and poverty in the UK, so that food banks can be consigned to the history books.

Sadly, hunger is only one area of injustice in our world. Homelessness, modern slavery and many other issues stem from injustices in our society. When Jesus quoted the prophet Isaiah, he gave us, his followers, a mandate to campaign for justice, setting people free from all types of oppression. Each of us can play a small part; together we can make a significant difference by giving, volunteering and campaigning.

Is there a cause close to your heart, where you are working with others to transform unjust structures of society? Subscribing to news updates and praying about the issues is a starting point. Writing to your MP or to the relevant government minister could be a next step. How about volunteering to use your skills with a favourite charity?

Pray for any charities you are already linked with, and next time you watch or listen to a news programme or read a newspaper, ask God to highlight an area where you can get involved in bringing hope and justice.

CATHERINE BUTCHER

Care for the planet

The Lord God took the man and put him in the garden of Eden to work it and take care of it. (NIV)

Ash dieback and Dutch elm disease have meant that many of the trees in and around Eastbourne, where I live, have been felled. In response, the local council and volunteers have been planting thousands of new trees, which will capture carbon and help tackle climate change. My husband has been one of the campaigners, contacting local churches and inviting them to plant trees on church land. The aim is for the town to be carbon neutral by 2030.

'Responding to climate change is an essential part of our responsibility to safeguard God's creation,' according to Justin Welby, archbishop of Canterbury.

The Genesis story reminds us that God made a good world, which we are commissioned to care for. We are also commanded to love God and to love our neighbours as ourselves, that includes our global neighbours whose livelihoods and land are being affected by climate change. For example, low-lying Pacific islands could disappear as sea levels rise – some have already vanished beneath the waves.

Around the world people are losing hope that climate change can be halted. In the face of fear and hopelessness, we are called to love. Caring for our planet is one way we can love our neighbours and be people of hope.

We can each respond in small ways as we become aware of our own habits which contribute to climate change. We can also challenge the practices in our workplace or the wider world, which are harming the environment.

In the past, some Christians have ignored environmental challenges, pointing to the fact that, when Jesus comes again, there will be a new heaven and a new earth. But that attitude ignores our current responsibility to care for our planet and to bring hope to humanity, with God's help.

Ask God's forgiveness for ways in which your habits have failed to care for the planet he has given us and failed to love our global neighbours. Invite him to show you how you can make a difference.

CATHERINE BUTCHER

The cloud of witnesses

Chris Leonard writes:

Earlier this month we celebrated Easter. Think of those first disciples, witnesses to the risen Jesus. That extraordinary experience transformed a fear-filled, despairing huddle into bold people of hope. Later, they told of what they had seen with their own eyes, spreading the gospel far and wide across the known world, often at great cost to themselves. After all, the Greek word sometimes translated as 'witness' is 'martyr'!

Jesus said to Thomas: 'Because you have seen me, you have believed; blessed are those who have not seen and yet have believed' (John 20:29 NIV). Like all those Paul mentions in Hebrews 11, we too are witnesses; therefore, as Jesus himself said, we are blessed. Though our eyes haven't seen the resurrected Jesus, we will have witnessed his transforming power and love at work. We're not alone in that. A great 'cloud' of people has gone before and will come after us – people from every tribe, tongue and nation, all witnesses to the salvation that God brings, through Jesus. We'll be thanking God for those who have borne witness to us in person or through means such as scripture or true-life stories.

For these next eight days we'll be looking at what (or whom) we trust and allow to be our influencers (in other words, witnesses), affecting our everyday lives and the ways we perceive truth about God. We look to Jesus first, of course, at what he did and at what he shows us of his Father. We'll think too about those whom we might influence, through our words or the way we live. Because such influencers are true witnesses, demonstrating that Jesus really is the way, the truth and the life.

Is all of this daunting? What if we're false witnesses or chicken out? How can we ever be adequate? As we look forward to Pentecost, the next big celebration in the church's calendar, let's take on board the twin promises of the risen Jesus, as recorded in Acts 1:8: 'You will receive power when the Holy Spirit comes on you; and you will be my witnesses in Jerusalem, and in all Judea and Samaria, and to the ends of the earth.'

In whom do we trust?

Idols are silver and gold, made by human hands. They have mouths, but cannot speak, eyes, but cannot see... Those who make them will be like them, and so will all who trust in them... You who fear him, trust in the Lord. (NIV)

We, of course, wouldn't dream of trusting idols – let alone following them. How foolish of primitive man to trust objects they'd made themselves! These days, American banknotes witness to what we Christians know is right: 'In God we trust.' But hang on: have we perhaps put our trust in our wealth, or that of our nation? Are we trusting primarily in economics – as the man filling his barns did in Jesus' parable (Luke 12:13–21)? The complex global economic systems that humankind has created militate uncontrollably against justice, creating huge deprivation and suffering for the majority but ridiculous wealth for a handful.

Perhaps we trust mainly in scientists and the truth they witness through their experiments? I'm so grateful for the amazing things scientists have discovered and some get the world out of trouble. But others unleash too much choice, too much power for humankind to handle. Scientists aren't gods, all-knowing or all-seeing.

Who are our 'influencers'? Now that's a word for today! In concept, 'influencers' aren't so different from our 'cloud of witnesses'. Do we trust and follow people on Twitter, Facebook or blogs, or maybe celebrities on TV? Some may well have a good, constructive influence but many appal me and lead their disciple-followers into some dreadful choices, attitudes and actions.

There have been times when I've idolised some friend who is walking and working with God. I've tried to be exactly like her. What's the harm in that? God's had to remind me that he didn't want a clone of her: he wanted me to reflect him, through the lens of myself, to others. That way, my 'witness' would reach, and perhaps influence, different groups of people.

Holy Spirit, would you search my heart? Do an audit of whatever and whoever really influences me. Help me realign where necessary and to put my trust in Jesus first. Amen

CHRIS LEONARD

Biblical witnesses that faith works

I do not have time to tell about Gideon, Barak, Samson and Jephthah, about David and Samuel and the prophets, who through faith conquered kingdoms, administered justice, and gained what was promised… whose weakness was turned to strength. (NIV)

There are many people today who don't believe God exists. Others see faith as something nice and comforting to have, almost on the level of a child's naïve belief in Father Christmas. Perhaps they mistake 'the power of positive thinking' for Jesus' power and love at work in someone's life. Yet Christians remain perhaps the most accessible witnesses to his being alive – a dependable, faithful, loving God who listens and becomes involved in the lives of people today who trust in him.

Written around 2,000 years ago, Hebrews 11 reminds Christian Jews of accounts dating back to the dawn of humanity. The Old Testament shows people's faith bearing witness to the reality and trustworthiness of God. Not one of these people was perfect. Many messed up, came to a bad end or suffered, but all helped take God's involvement with humanity forwards. The beginning of this chapter says: 'Faith is confidence in what we hope for and assurance about what we do not see. This is what the ancients were commended for' (v. 1). Are you always confident of the hope you have in God and assured about what you do not see? I'm not. I doubt him sometimes, especially when prayers go seemingly unanswered, when he doesn't seem to be there, when everything is going wrong or when someone betrays my trust.

That's when stories from the Old and New Testament speak most powerfully across nations, cultures and time to confirm or witness to God being real and doing what he says he does. These stories show I'm not alone; this isn't something I've imagined; faith in God does work! Crucially, it's not about my strong faith in God: it's about our God, who turns human weakness to strength as we trust in him.

Who from this chapter 'witnesses' to (or 'influences') you most at this time? You might want to spend some time reflecting on and talking to God about their story – and yours.

CHRIS LEONARD

Cloud of witnesses

Therefore, since we are surrounded by such a great cloud of witnesses, let us throw off everything that hinders and the sin that so easily entangles. And let us run with perseverance the race marked out for us, fixing our eyes on Jesus, the pioneer and perfecter of faith. (NIV)

The 'therefore' that starts this passage refers to all the witnesses we met in Hebrews 11. The word translated 'cloud' here means, quite literally, cloud – plus, figuratively, 'a lot, a large number of'. Forget crowds of people floating in the sky! In the Bible, clouds are often a sign of God's veiled presence – as in the pillar of cloud, the cloud over Mount Sinai and the one hiding Jesus from the disciples' sight as he ascended into heaven. So it is that the faith-filled people of Hebrews 11, together with all such who lived before us, point the way to the presence of a God who remains invisible to most mortal eyes. Multitudes of these witnesses surround us. The word here can mean 'clothe'. Indeed, the Passion Translation says: 'As for us, we have all of these great witnesses who encircle [clothe] us like clouds' (Hebrews 12:1, TPT). I find that encouraging!

Abraham, Jacob, Esau and Rahab the prostitute, portrayed with all their faults in the Bible, are in this cloud – despite being unlikely characters to serve as evidence of God's presence. Maybe you and I are also clothed with God's presence? Though veiled, his presence in and around us may still be visible to those with eyes to see. 'Surely not!' you may say of yourself. But then haven't you known ordinary, humble Christians who have shone with God's presence at times, even though they would never have believed it of themselves?

We'll think more later about some of those people we've known, as well as those in the Bible. And, of course, of Jesus who is the ultimate witness, along with his promised Holy Spirit.

Lord, help me to walk today encircled and clothed by all these encouraging witnesses to your presence – and ultimately by Jesus himself. Amen

CHRIS LEONARD

Ordinary witnesses, extraordinary consequences

A disciple named Tabitha (in Greek her name is Dorcas)… was always doing good and helping the poor… [When] she became ill and died… [Peter] took her by the hand and helped her to her feet… This became known all over Joppa, and many people believed in the Lord. (NIV)

In my sewing kit is a tin of pins, trademarked 'Dorcas'. Mum bought it for me for when we had needlework lessons at the start of secondary school. Why 'Dorcas' as a make of dressmakers' pins? Because in a Bible story this very ordinary woman sewed clothes for the poor. The widows of her town loved her and were clearly devastated when she died. Then something extraordinary happened – Peter came, he prayed and God raised Dorcas from the dead! Peter 'called for the believers, especially the widows, and presented her to them alive' (v. 41). Imagine what witnessing that did for their faith! As the widows, including Dorcas herself, spread the word, many more came to faith in Jesus in that town and Peter stayed on to teach them more.

Now, whenever I use my pins, I'm reminded of this good woman, who followed Jesus and did what she could to help others. There is even an international Christian charity named after her. They 'stand for justice and peace… As the worst humanitarian crises of our time persist, we work to deliver lasting change for people at the heart of it.' And so, Dorcas' (Tabitha's) story, that of an ordinary, faithful disciple of Jesus doing good in practical ways, lives on.

Dorcas' story reminds me of a woman in our church who would consider herself ordinary, but serves faithfully in loving, practical ways. She told me of the recent funeral of a man who had led her church youth group, decades earlier. 'He wasn't much older than we were, but there are six couples in different churches around the country today, still in touch and still living for Jesus because of that youth leader's influence.'

Lord, help us to see how serving others for you in practical, everyday ways can open doors to people's hearts and point them to you. Sometimes you multiply our small efforts – and we may never know the full effect. Thank you! Amen
CHRIS LEONARD

Parents, grandparents, ancestors

To Timothy, my dear son… I thank God, whom I serve, as my ancestors did… I am reminded of your sincere faith, which first lived in your grandmother Lois and in your mother Eunice and, I am persuaded, now lives in you also. (NIV)

Do you, like me, ever think wryly that you're turning into your mother as you grow older? Parents and grandparents are undoubtedly an influence on our lives, for good or ill. My parents and grandparents were all Christians. Each acted as part of my personal 'cloud of witnesses' to Jesus – introducing me to him before I can remember. Each did so in their own individual way because every person and every relationship is different. I'm not anyone's clone, I have my own relationship with Jesus, but I thank God for those family witnesses who influenced me from the very start of my life.

Paul had recognised something in Timothy, something he'd seen, out-worked in a more mature way perhaps, in the young man's mother and grandmother, Eunice and Lois. Through their relationship with Jesus, they bore witness to Timothy that Jesus lives and loves and saves. Young Timothy saw faith at work and followed Jesus in his turn. In those early days of the church, to find three generations of a family bearing witness to new life in Jesus must have gladdened Paul's heart too.

Generations, biological or not, are important to God throughout scripture. Paul's Jewish ancestors witnessed to faith in God. Paul calls Timothy 'my dear son' (v. 2). After years of being a very special witness and mentor to him, Paul, imprisoned and facing execution, charges Timothy with carrying on his work. Maybe you're the first in your family to know God. Were you 'parented' in the faith by someone outside of your biological family who became the first in your 'cloud of witnesses'?

Thank you, Lord, for those both within and outside my biological family who witnessed to, and parented me, in Christ. Help me to parent and witness to others, especially across the generations. Amen

CHRIS LEONARD

Everyday witness

Your faith in Christ Jesus and… the love you have for all God's people… spring from the hope stored up for you in heaven and… the gospel that… is bearing fruit and growing… since… you learned it from Epaphras. (NIV)

I was going through a bit of a teenage 'thing' and couldn't seem to talk to my mum. Then a woman in our church took me under her wing. I can't have known Phyll for more than a couple of years in total, but she gave me time, let me talk and was a faithful witness who influenced and encouraged me in the Lord.

I've been immensely impressed reading about extraordinary Christians like Brother Andrew and Corrie ten Boom, but somehow, it's the 'ordinary', loving Christians like Phyll who show me how to walk with Jesus day by day. Much later I wrote a series of books featuring some of these 'ordinary' Christians. It's often easier to relate to them than to famous ones like saints, bishops or founders of great works.

During the long periods of the Covid-19 lockdowns, when churches couldn't meet, I so missed seeing the people in my usual congregation – the ones who endured through all life's ups and downs, serving and worshipping so faithfully.

Paul, isolated in prison, is writing to 'God's holy people in Colossae, the faithful brothers and sisters in Christ' (v. 2). We don't know their names or much about them, and yet their faithful witness to Christ has come to Paul's attention and encouraged him. Epaphras, who witnessed to the Colossians initially, only appears outside of this letter in Philemon 1:23, as one of Paul's fellow prisoners.

So many names appear in the Bible: so many unnamed characters too. According to 1 Corinthians 15:6, the resurrected Jesus 'appeared to more than five hundred of the brothers and sisters at the same time'. Billions since then have shown or witnessed to their own experience of his being still alive and active.

Lord, may the quality of my faith and of the love I have for people grow ever more like yours. May my faith shine out amid my everyday life, as witness to your resurrection life and love in me. Amen

CHRIS LEONARD

The other side of the coin

The Lord preserves the simple; when I was brought low, he saved me. Return, O my soul, to your rest; for the Lord has dealt bountifully with you... I believed, even when I spoke: 'I am greatly afflicted'; I said in my alarm, 'All mankind are liars.' (ESV)

The writer of this psalm doesn't lie when he says he is afflicted and brought low. His emotions swing from one extreme to another, as though he's on some nightmarish fairground ride. And isn't that what can happen when we're in acute distress – having experienced terror, extreme pain or betrayal? By calling on God to save him, the psalmist shows that he does still believe in and trust God – otherwise why would he sing to him so honestly of his struggles and his pain? Yet in his anguish and 'alarm' he declares, 'All mankind are liars' (v. 11) – in other words, he has lost any ability to trust people. So much for the cloud of (human) witnesses now! If he sees them all as false, there is a danger that his pain will harden into cynicism, isolation, bitterness and desire for revenge. Maybe these are the 'bonds' from which God frees him as he determines to serve the Lord (v. 16).

If we are looking at the cloud of amazing witnesses to God, we have to acknowledge that some are, or become, false. False Christian witnesses cause real damage – they might be dishonest in financial matters or dictatorial, embrace a heresy or another church member's wife, or abuse children. If, for example, it was your child who was abused, your spouse gone, your church split or your generous giving over the years misappropriated, then I think this psalm would speak to you.

Perhaps you know people who still love God but won't go anywhere near church because past hurt caused them to lose trust in human witnesses to Christ. I think this psalm provides deep understanding of someone in this position, together with hope and even strategy for how to come through, with God's help.

Lord, we pray for those whose trust has been betrayed by those who previously influenced them. Will you break their chains, heal their hurt and confusion, and restore their love for people and for yourself? Amen

CHRIS LEONARD

Jesus

Let those who fear the Lord say: 'His love endures forever'… I was pushed back and about to fall, but the Lord helped me. The Lord is my strength and my defence; he has become my salvation… The stone the builders rejected has become the cornerstone. (NIV)

I happened to be reading Psalm 118 while I was writing these notes. It seemed to shed further light on the words we've been considering all week: 'Since we are surrounded by such a great cloud of witnesses, let us throw off everything that hinders and the sin that so easily entangles. And let us run with perseverance the race marked out for us, fixing our eyes on Jesus, the pioneer and perfecter of faith' (Hebrews 12:1–2). I challenge you, before you read on with today's note, to consider Psalm 118 in the light of Jesus' influence on your own life. Then see if you agree with my summary of its practical instructions below.

Let all who follow the Lord witness to his love that endures forever. Trust in him, not politicians. Cut down, in the Lord's name, whatever hinders. Treat your own bad attitudes, actions and thought patterns as enemies. If we fall, he is our help and defence, our Saviour from whom our strength comes. He will chasten us sometimes, but he promises that Jesus, who pioneered our faith, will perfect it if we persevere, keeping our eyes fixed on him. Ultimately, it's Jesus' righteousness alone that allows the gate to open, inviting us to enter and sit in the very presence of God.

Note too those amazing, prophetic words: 'The stone the builders rejected has become the cornerstone' (v. 22). The church is 'built on the foundation of the apostles and prophets, with Christ Jesus himself as the chief cornerstone. In him the whole building is joined together and rises to become a holy temple in the Lord' (Ephesians 2:20–21). We're not left with only a nebulous, sometimes unreliable, cloud of witnesses. Instead, Jesus himself gives us sure alignment and focus.

Lord, as individuals, local churches and the whole great 'cloud' of your witnesses, may we run with perseverance the great race marked out for us, fixing our eyes on you, the pioneer and perfecter of our faith. Amen

CHRIS LEONARD

Enabling all ages to grow in faith

Anna Chaplaincy
Living Faith
Messy Church
Parenting for Faith

BRF is a Christian charity that resources individuals and churches. Our vision is to enable people of all ages to grow in faith and understanding of the Bible and to see more people equipped to exercise their gifts in leadership and ministry.

To find out more about our work, visit

brf.org.uk

Lent is traditionally a time of repentance, fasting and prayer as we prepare to celebrate our salvation at Easter. Through daily readings and reflections from Ash Wednesday to Easter Day, Amy Scott Robinson explores different biblical images of repentance, sin, forgiveness and grace, bringing them together in Holy Week as a lens through which to view Christ's work of reconciliation on the cross.

Images of Grace
A journey from darkness to light at Easter
Amy Scott Robinson
978 1 80039 117 8 £9.99
brfonline.org.uk

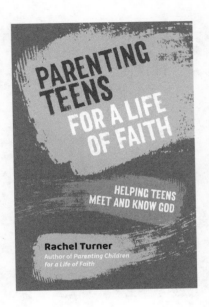

Parenting teens has its challenges and it can be easy to think we are less influential in their lives, particularly when it comes to faith. But that is not true. Parents remain the significant spiritual influencer in a teen's life, and they need us to help them navigate the world and faith together. This book will help all parents, carers, grandparents and others involved in teens' everyday lives to understand the teenage faith journey more and find their place within it.

Parenting Teens for a Life of Faith
Helping teens meet and know God
Rachel Turner
978 1 80039 163 5 £9.99
brfonline.org.uk

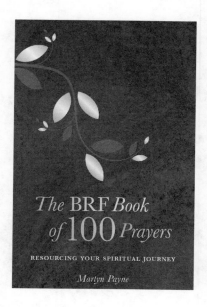

Prayer is at the heart of BRF's work, and this special illustrated anniversary collection is a celebration of prayer for BRF's centenary year. It can be used in a range of different settings, from individual devotions to corporate worship. Including sections on prayers of preparation, seasonal prayers, and themed prayers for special times and hard times, it is the perfect daily companion to resource your spiritual journey.

The BRF Book of 100 Prayers
Resourcing your spiritual journey
Martyn Payne
978 1 80039 147 5   £12.99
brfonline.org.uk

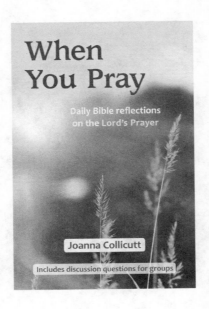

In this updated edition of a classic text, Joanna Collicutt shows how growing as a Christian is rooted in the prayer Jesus gave us. As we pray the Lord's Prayer, we express our relationship with God, absorb gospel values and are also motivated to live them out. As we pray to the Father, in union with the Son, through the power of the Spirit, so we begin to take on the character of Christ.

When You Pray
Daily Bible reflections on the Lord's Prayer
Joanna Collicutt
978 0 85746 867 3 £10.99
brfonline.org.uk

To order

Online: **brfonline.org.uk**
Telephone: +44 (0)1865 319700
Mon–Fri 9.30–17.00

Delivery times within the UK are normally 15 working days. Prices are correct at the time of going to press but may change without prior notice.

Title	Price	Qty	Total
Images of Grace	£9.99		
Parenting Teens for a Life of Faith	£9.99		
The BRF Book of 100 Prayers	£12.99		
When You Pray	£10.99		

POSTAGE AND PACKING CHARGES			
Order value	UK	Europe	Rest of world
Under £7.00	£2.00		
£7.00–£29.99	£3.00	Available on request	Available on request
£30.00 and over	FREE		

Total value of books	
Donation	
Postage and packing	
Total for this order	

Please complete in BLOCK CAPITALS

Title .... First name/initials .... Surname ....

Address ....

.... Postcode ....

Acc. No. .... Telephone ....

Email ....

Method of payment

❑ Cheque (made payable to BRF) ❑ MasterCard / Visa

Card no. ▢▢▢▢ ▢▢▢▢ ▢▢▢▢ ▢▢▢▢ ▢▢▢▢ ▢▢▢▢

Expires end ▢▢ M M ▢▢ Y Y   Security code ▢▢▢   Last 3 digits on the reverse of the card

We will use your personal data to process this order. From time to time we may send you information about the work of BRF. Please contact us if you wish to discuss your mailing preferences **brf.org.uk/privacy**

Please return this form to:

BRF, 15 The Chambers, Vineyard, Abingdon OX14 3FE | enquiries@brf.org.uk

For terms and cancellation information, please visit **brfonline.org.uk/terms**.

Bible Reading Fellowship (BRF) is a charity (233280) and company limited by guarantee (301324), registered in England and Wales

Each issue of *Day by Day with God* is available from Christian bookshops everywhere. Copies may also be available through your church book agent or from the person who distributes Bible reading notes in your church.

Alternatively you may obtain *Day by Day with God* on subscription direct from the publishers. There are two kinds of subscription:

Individual subscriptions

covering 3 issues for 4 copies or less, payable in advance
(including postage & packing).

To order, please complete the details on page 144 and return with the appropriate payment to: BRF, 15 The Chambers, Vineyard, Abingdon OX14 3FE

You can also use the form on page 144 to order a gift subscription for a friend.

Group subscriptions

covering 3 issues for 5 copies or more, sent to one UK address (post free).

Please note that the annual billing period for group subscriptions runs from 1 May to 30 April.

To order, please complete the details on page 143 and return with the appropriate payment to: BRF, 15 The Chambers, Vineyard, Abingdon OX14 3FE

You will receive an invoice with the first issue of notes.

All our Bible reading notes can be ordered online by visiting
brfonline.org.uk/collections/subscriptions

Day by Day with God is also available as
an app for Android, iPhone and iPad
brfonline.org.uk/collections/apps

All subscription enquiries should be directed to:
BRF, 15 The Chambers, Vineyard, Abingdon OX14 3FE
+44 (0)1865 319700 | **enquiries@brf.org.uk**

DBDWG0123